the SECRET WEAPON

TEACHING KIDS TO PRAY

Tina Houser

Warner Press Kids™
educate • nurture • inspire
www.warnerpress.org

THE SECRET WEAPON
TEACHING KIDS TO PRAY
        by Tina Houser

©2012 by Warner Press Inc Anderson, IN 46018
www.warnerpress.com

ISBN: 978-1-59317-440-8

Editors: Karen Rhodes, Robin Fogle
Design & Illustrations: Curt Corzine/Christian Elden/Kevin Spear
Printed in USA

Warner Press Kids™
educate • nurture • inspire
www.warnerpress.org

Contents

DEDICATION

With gratitude...

This book, along with the speaking engagements and all the other things I find myself in the middle of, could not happen without the never-ceasing support of my husband, Ray. Thank you, Honey, for fielding my theological questions, for packing the car and unpacking the car, for openly being a proud husband, for taking me to see grandbabies when I need to be in my "happy place", for packing and unpacking the car, for protecting me when I'm trying to do something I shouldn't be, for packing and unpacking the car, and for reminding me every morning that you love me.

Thank you to my son, Jarad, who honors me more than I deserve...who challenges me spiritually...who exposes me to the way a different generation thinks and reacts to the Word...who pushes his technologically-challenged mom to use the tools available in this cyber world...who opens his home anytime I need a place to work and play...who makes me a better person for being around him...who celebrates with me...who makes me proud on a whole new level.

And, thank you to Karen Rhodes, Regina Jackson and all those at Warner Press who believe in what I do and who are committed to providing tools for children's ministry workers so they can reach little ones for God's Kingdom. Thank you for the opportunities to share the ideas that God passes through my crazy little brain!

tina!

For the rest of the story, see page 18.

v

INTRODUCTION

The Secret Weapon: Teaching Kids to Pray

In Ephesians 6:10-18 we find a description of the armor of God, but most of us remember it only through verse 17. We talk about the belt of truth, the breastplate of righteousness, the shoes of peace, the shield of faith, and the helmet of salvation. But, verse 18 tells us about our Secret Weapon—prayer! It encourages us to have this weapon with us at all times and on every occasion. This is the weapon that clobbers the enemy and leaves him wondering what in the world hit him.

Too often we think of prayer as being quiet, with our hands folded reverently. But, if we view prayer as a vital weapon in our arsenal against Satan, maybe we need to rethink that "quiet" stuff. James 5:16 tells us that God's power is released through fervent prayer… fervent. "Fervent" brings to mind words like bold, intense, zealous, and impassioned. That sure doesn't sound quiet to me!

God knows the armor He has given us is the equipment we need to defeat the hold our enemy has on our friends, family, neighbors, country and world. When we pull out the Secret Weapon, Satan trembles and runs for cover.

In the pages of this book you'll find lots of ways for kids to use their Secret Weapon. The activities are intended to tap into multiple intelligences so kids can experience fervent prayer and understand the potential of their Secret Weapon. I challenge you to experiment with some of these prayer ideas, even if they feel a little out of your comfort zone. The Bible clearly shows us that prayer is sometimes physical, sometimes loud, sometimes desperate. If the Bible is our guide, then let's give it a chance to speak into our lives. I hope as you experience prayer in new ways you will be inspired to create other ways that will help you and your children connect and communicate with our Heavenly Father. May His kingdom come and His will be done!

tina!

A PRAYER WARRIOR

During the first year of marriage, my RA (rheumatoid arthritis) was in high gear. My goal each day was to clean one room of our 2-bedroom apartment…that's it. My hands swelled so badly that twice my wedding and engagement rings cut through the skin on my finger and had to be cut off. They haven't been on for more than a few minutes since.

During that time, a lady from church, Jackie, invited us to accompany her family to the Los Angeles County Fair. Ray tactfully explained that he didn't think I would be able to handle the night out, even though he knew I loved the fair. Jackie suggested we make tentative plans and wait to see how I felt on Friday.

Each day that week I felt a little bit stronger, and then Friday started out better than any day I could remember in months. Ray and I couldn't believe what we were saying, but we accepted the invitation to dinner and the fair. A prime rib dinner started our evening, which isn't a bad start for anything if you ask me. At the fair we walked, we laughed, we rode the rides, and we spent rolls upon rolls of dimes trying to win 50-cent stuffed animals. It was a night to remember!

In all honesty, I have to say that the next day I paid dearly for it, but we had to wonder where the pain went for those six hours. Arthur (as we referred to my RA) had disappeared for the evening… yeah, no sign of him.

The next week Ray had the opportunity to talk with Jackie and express his gratitude for the evening once again. He told her that even though it had been quite tiring, it was a paradise in the middle of a lot of pain. Jackie responded with a confident, but far from arrogant, "I knew she would have a good night." She hesitantly went on to say that after her invitation to the fair on Sunday, she decided to spend the week fasting and praying for just one relaxed, pain-free evening for me. For an entire week she had gone without food in order to concentrate all her thoughts and energy on petitioning the Lord for my night out. She made a totally selfless request of the Lord on my behalf. She didn't announce it to anyone and was a little reluctant to tell Ray. But it had been a wonderful spiritual experience for her and she wanted to share it with us. As it turned out, through her sharing, the night at the Los Angeles County Fair became a spiritual treasure of encouragement and endearment.

To this day, every time I think of the gift Jackie gave me—a prayer that for one night I would be physically whole—I am challenged to give more completely of myself for others. Although she now enjoys walking with Jesus, Jackie exemplified a life that relies on the power of prayer.

Alphabet Thankfulness Prayer

Objective: To help kids keep their eyes open and pay attention to the things around them that God created.

Materials
- 26 pieces of cardstock
- Pencils
- Timer

Before You Begin...
1. Write each letter of the alphabet on a separate piece of cardstock.
2. Post the cards around the room. They do not need to be in alphabetical order; in fact, it might be more fun if they're not.

Prayer Time
- The kids will think of things that God created and write them on the card representing the first letter of that object. (Example: cliffs would go on the "C" card, and dandelions would go on the "D" card.)
- Set a timer at 5 minutes and see how many things the kids can come up with. If their object is already written on the letter card, then they need to think of something different.
- At the end of the 5 minutes, the kids will choose a letter card. The card they choose will be part of their thankfulness prayer.

Teachable Moments
Everything comes from the hand of God. It may be made in a factory, but the "stuff" it's made of was created by God. When you trace it back to its very beginning, God was there, making the ingredients!

The kids will take turns thanking God for the things on their letter card by saying, "Thank You, God, for _____ because they are _____." We take so many things for granted, like blades of grass, the wind, an umbrella on a rainy day, and Bandaids™ to cover our boo-boos. This prayer exercise will help kids keep their eyes open and pay attention (a little more) to the things around them they assume will always be there.

God Speaks:
Devote yourselves to prayer with an alert mind and a thankful heart. Colossians 4:2 (NLT)

Altar Prayer

Objective: To teach kids what an altar is and how it is used.

Materials
- ½-gallon milk or juice cartons
- Adhesive shelf paper
- Duct tape
- Large cookie sheet

Before You Begin...
1. Gather a large supply of ½-gallon milk or juice cartons. Clean and dry them thoroughly.
2. Fold the top into the carton so the end is flat. Use duct tape to keep it in place. The carton should now be a rectangular box.
3. Adhesive shelf paper comes in a lot of different patterns, many of them have a granite or marble design. Use these patterned adhesive papers to cover the cartons.
4. Now, you have a great supply of building blocks that will come in handy more than you can even imagine right now!

Teachable Moments & Prayer Time

The kids will construct an altar from the covered cartons. When it is done, place a large cookie sheet upside down on the top. The kids will kneel around this altar to pray. Kneeling at this altar—right here in their room—will help ease their fear of going to the altar in your church. Use this opportunity to also teach about the altar and what it is for.

Prayer can involve something physical, like kneeling at an altar. Sitting in a comfortable chair with your hands folded can become routine and assumed. When you move your body and get out of your comfort zone, your mind is more attentive to what is taking place.

Take the children to the altar in your church. **Ask:**
- What have you noticed about this altar?
- What is it used for?
- What happens at the altar?

People come to the altar to pray about special needs in their lives. Maybe they are going through something difficult and want to ask God for His help and guidance in getting through it. People come to pray for others they know and care about. They also come to pray at the altar when they want to ask God to forgive them for leading a life that has not been pleasing to Him. Sometimes, people come to the altar to pray for healing.

Because the church is a family of believers, others from the congregation may come to the altar to pray with them. The pastor may anoint the person with oil. To anoint means to set someone apart. When the person is anointed, their situation is set apart, and the people concentrate their prayers on that one special need. There is no special power in the oil; it is a symbol of God's power.

God Speaks:
Are any of you sick? You should call for the elders of the church to come and pray over you, anointing you with oil in the name of the Lord. James 5:14 (NLT)

Backpack Prayers

**Objective: To meet the physical needs of others less fortunate
while supporting and encouraging them in prayer.**

Materials
- Backpacks
- Note paper
- Pencils
- Ribbon
- School supplies

Start planning in July or August!

Before You Begin...

1. An absolutely wonderful service project for kids is to collect backpacks filled with school supplies. Your kids will have a keen connection with this project. Run the backpack round-up during the last part of July and through August when supplies are super-cheap in the discount department stores. Challenge the kids to bring in miscellaneous school supplies or even fill a backpack that matches the one they are preparing for themselves.
2. Contact the local school system to arrange the distribution. Usually, the counselor will keep the backpacks and distribute them without you knowing who they went to. That protects the feelings of the children receiving the backpacks.
3. On the final day of your backpack drive, hopefully you will have enough backpacks that each child will be able to put one on during prayer. If not, several children can gather around a backpack and place their hands on it.

Prayer Time

- Each child will pray aloud for the student who will receive the supplies he has on his back. If the child has a difficult time praying out loud, then he can repeat a simple prayer after you.
- Before returning the backpack, the child should write a note to the student, even though she won't know his or her name. In the note she should let the recipient know that he or she has been prayed for and will continue to be prayed for. Also, encourage the recipients to use the supplies to do well so they will honor God.
- Lastly, give each child a ribbon to tie to the backpack that he or she will carry this year. Each time they see the ribbon, they should pray that God will encourage and watch over the child who received their backpack.

God Speaks:

This is my command: Love each other. John 15:17 (NIV)

Be a Friend Prayer

Objective: To learn to pray for our friends who need the Lord.

Materials

- 1 piece of black poster board (4" x 4")
- chalk
- flashlight
- pieces of black construction paper (about 4" x 4")

Teachable Moments

The Bible tells us to pray for one another. James 5:16 (NIrV) says *Pray for one another so that you might be healed. The prayer of a godly person is powerful. It makes things happen.* What does this verse say to you? We pray so our friends will have their souls healed. It says that prayer is powerful and that it makes things happen! That's pretty dog-gone exciting! Talk to God about your friends who need to know the Lord. Tell Him how badly you want your friends to have what you have. Ask Him to make you a good influence and example. Ask God to show you how you can ASSIST your friends in knowing Jesus.

Mark 2:1-12 tells us the story of a paralyzed man who was brought to Jesus by his four friends. There was no way for them to get the man into the house where Jesus was because of the crowd, so they cut a hole in the roof and lowered the man down in front of Jesus. When Jesus healed the man, He said that it was the faith of the man's friends that made the man well. Praying for your friends… having faith for your friends…is important!

Prayer Time

- Using the chalk, write the word "Friend" on the piece of black poster board. Lay the black poster board over the end of the flashlight so the kids can see the word "Friend." Turn out the lights and notice that the light has to stay on one side of the poster board because it has no way to go through.

- Poke a hole in the poster board with a sharp pencil. This hole represents you praying for your friend. Now, hold the poster board over the flashlight and turn out the lights. A stream of light comes through the hole. Our prayer is getting through to our friend.

- Now, let's poke another hole through the poster board. Hold it over the flashlight and turn out the lights. Each time we poke another hole more light comes through. Each time we pray for our friends, we're praying that they will see more of God. Each time we pray, it cuts through the darkness in their lives. Remember, prayer is powerful and can make things happen!

- Give each child a piece of black construction paper and access to some chalk. Do you have a friend who needs to know that they can have their sins forgiven and their soul healed? Do you have a friend who needs to know how to get to Jesus? Do you have a friend who needs you to assist by praying for her? Write the name of that person on your black paper using the chalk.

- Hold on to your paper with your friend's name on it and let's pray for him or her right now.

  Lead the children in praying for their friends. Start the prayer by having each child say his or her friend's name as the prayer opens. "Lord, my friend _____ needs to know you…"

God Speaks:

Seeing their faith, Jesus said to the paralyzed man, "My child, your sins are forgiven." Mark 2:5 (NLT)

Breathing

Objective: To help kids understand that praying in God's presence is as important as breathing in air.

Materials
- "Breathe," the song by Michael W. Smith
- Stop watch

Before You Begin...
1. Is breathing important? Let's see how important breathing really is.
2. Time how long it takes each child to go without breathing. One way to do this, so it's more obvious, is to have them hum without taking a breath. Or, you may want the kids to pinch their noses and lips tightly.
3. Record the times.

Teachable Moments
What happens when we stop breathing completely? Breathing is pretty important, isn't it? Breathing is like praying. Praying is pretty important, too. Breathing keeps your bodies alive, and prayer keeps our souls alive. Our bodies won't forget to breathe, but we sometimes forget to pray. When we start forgetting to pray often, we get further and further away from God. It's as if we don't know Him anymore. Pray often, and keep breathing.

Listen to "Breathe" by Michael W. Smith. You can download YouTube videos of different artists singing this beautiful song. Lyrics can also be printed from the Internet.

Prayer Time
- How is prayer like breathing? How is prayer like your daily bread? What feeling do you get when you can't get enough air? How is that feeling of not having enough air like prayer? What do you think of when you hear the word "desperate"?
- Lead the kids in prayer, but after each sentence, pause.
    - During that pause, instruct everyone to take one nice…slow…deliberate… breath to completely fill his or her lungs.
    - Pray another sentence and pause for another deep breath.
- How did it feel to completely fill your lungs with fresh air each time you took a deep breath?
- Through prayer we "inhale" God, because we come into His presence. Praying should be as natural to a God-follower as breathing is, and much more satisfying!

God Speaks:
I can never escape from your Spirit! I can never get away from your presence! Psalm 139:7 (NLT)

Chop-Chop Prayer

Objective: To discuss what tempts kids to turn from the Lord, and how to commit to Him and stay committed.

Materials
- Heavy yarn
- Scissors

Before You Begin...

1. Cut three pieces of thick yarn, about a foot long, for each child.
2. Hold them so the ends are together and then make a knot in the end. This should look like three strands of hair. The kids will make a braid from these three strands before moving into prayer.
3. During prayer, each child will also need a pair of scissors.

Teachable Moments

When Samson's hair was cut, his strength was gone. When he shared the secret of his strength, he went against his commitment and dedication to the Lord. Samson was strong physically, but his commitment wasn't so strong. Just like Samson, each day you have to choose whether you are going to stay strong in your commitment to the Lord or if you are going to fall for Satan's temptations. Satan knows where your weaknesses are, and he will try to wear you down, just like he wore down Samson.

The kids will name things that tempt them to turn away from the Lord. These can include things like: friends, sports, hobbies, video games, habits, schoolwork, and family relationships.

Prayer Time
- As the kids pray, they will hold on to their braid and scissors.
- Pray about one thing they have listed that tempts them to turn away from the Lord.
- Each child will have to do a self-evaluation. If the one thing just prayed about represents something that pulls him away from his commitment to the Lord, then the child should cut off a piece of the yarn braid. Then, pray for the next temptation listed.
- When you allow these things to mess up your commitment to the Lord, then you become spiritually weak. The good news is that God can restore your strength! God can give you new strength when you admit you've relied on the wrong things for strength.
- Is your braid chopped up pretty badly? God can give you new strength when you make a new commitment to Him. It will be like starting over with a new braid. This time, don't let Satan trick you into falling for his temptations!

God Speaks:

When you are tempted he will show you a way out so that you will not give in to it.
   1 Corinthians 10:13 (NLT)

Cover One Another

Objective: To help kids learn how to "cover" their friends in prayer.

Materials
- Bar magnet
- Paper clip

Before You Begin...

Look up and read James 5:16: *Confess your sins to each other and PRAY for each other so that you may be healed. The earnest PRAYER of a righteous person has great power and produces wonderful results. (NLT)*

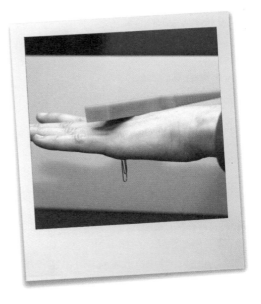

Teachable Moments

Involve the children in a simple experiment.
- Place a paper clip on a flat surface. Cover it with the child's hand. Make sure his or her hand is flat against the surface and that the paper clip is under the ball of his or her palm.
- Position the bar magnet across the back of his or her hand (the knuckles). The magnet should be directly above the paper clip.
- The child will slowly raise his or her hand while you hold the magnet against the knuckles.
- The paper clip will hang from the palm of the hand.

Prayer Time

Let's say the paper clip is someone who needs us to pray for him or her. Give your paper clip a name—someone you want to pray for. James 5:16 says that our prayers should be "earnest." That means we really, really mean it! We should cover that person with prayer…pray for him or her a whole bunch, not just once a week.

When you place your hand over your paper clip (the person you're praying for) that represents how you are covering him or her in prayer. Your hand is completely covering your paper clip. You pray for him or her when you get up in the morning. You pray for him or her when you see his or her favorite TV show. You pray for him or her when you see someone who looks like him or her. You pray for him or her every time his or her name pops into your mind.

Prayer is like a blanket that you completely cover them with. When you cover them in prayer, you lift them to God. How amazing is that! When you lifted your hand, the paper clip came with it. Let that remind you of how your prayers lift others to God. James 5:16 says that prayer has great power.

God Speaks:

See James 5:16 above.

Depend on One Another

Objective: To show kids the importance of supporting each other in prayer.

Before You Begin...
1. As your brother or your sister in Christ, I want you to depend on me to pray for you.
2. We should also depend on one another for support through prayer.

Teachable Moments
You can do an exercise that will show how we support one another physically. The kids will make a circle and interlock their arms at the elbow.

Everyone should plant his or her heels in the floor and then gently lean back. As long as everyone holds on to his neighbors, the entire circle will lean back and no one will fall.

Prayer Time
- The children will stand in a tight circle with their arms over one another's shoulders.
- YOU may have to get down on your knees so the children will be able to lay their arms over your shoulders.
- We need to support one another, especially when we're trying to stand up for what we believe God would have us do.
- The children can share current situations where they need the support of friends.
- As each situation is mentioned, pray as group to support that person.

God Speaks
Finally, all of you, live in harmony with one another; be sympathetic, love as brothers, and be compassionate and humble. 1 Peter 3:8 (NIV)

Ears to Better Hear

Objective: To help kids realize ways they can "hear" God speaking to them.

Materials
- Costume rubber ears

Teachable Moments

Put the rubber ears on as you begin to talk with the children about prayer. At first, they will giggle and make remarks about the ears. Then ask: Why do you think I'm wearing these ears? Does it make you think I'm having trouble hearing? Maybe if my ears were bigger, I could hear God speak! Have you ever heard the voice of God? Me neither! But I have felt God's presence and His direction in a very real way. It's not by putting on these big ears, though.

Instead of putting on jumbo rubber ears, there are some things that we can do that will help us hear what God is trying to tell us. Is it easier to hear what someone's saying in a quiet restaurant or in a restaurant where there's singing and bells clanging and a party going on?

It's the same with listening to God. When you quiet yourself…calm down…take a deep breath… no TV or music…then you're more likely to understand what God wants you to know. The other thing about hearing is that you need to close your mouth. We get busy in our prayer time telling God all the things that we're concerned about and would like His help with, and then we say "amen."

There wasn't any time for listening. Stop using your mouth so much and listen…but not with your jumbo rubber ears! Instead of listening with your ears, listen with your heart.

Prayer Time
- Have you ever seen someone hurting and wondered what you could do to help?
- When there's a situation that really breaks your heart, God will speak to your broken heart and help you figure out what you can do to serve those people.
- Pray together about the things the children mentioned that cause their hearts to break.
- Then, ask the children to cup their hands around their ears as if listening more intently.
- Spend a few minutes in quiet, keeping all other thoughts out of their heads and concentrating on what they have just mentioned in prayer.

God Speaks:

But don't just listen to God's word. You must do what it says. Otherwise, you are only fooling yourselves. James 1:22 (NLT)

Eggshell Prayers

Objective: To teach kids how prayer will help make them strong enough to forgive.

Materials
- Cracked egg
- Eggshells
- Fine tip permanent markers
- Small drop cloth

Teachable Moments

Children and adults are quick to talk about how others have offended them, hurt their feelings, or done something that spoiled the relationship. They talk, talk, talk about it as if there is no solution.

The solution is forgiveness, but forgiving or asking for forgiveness is never easy. We don't like to talk about the things that we know we should do, but aren't doing. Forgiveness…where you clean up the relationship and put the wrong in the past never to bring it up again…takes God's power. It's takes prayer power! God will give the words and the tender heart.

Prayer Time
- Place the drop cloth where you'll be talking. **Say**, "Always open the egg carton at the store to make sure that none of the eggs are cracked. A cracked egg won't do me any good when I start to make a cake. "
- Show the cracked egg. When we refuse to forgive someone, it's like an egg that has a broken shell. Something is not right. The relationship is not how it is supposed to be. An unforgiving attitude breaks families and friends apart, just as this eggshell has been broken apart.
- Pull the egg apart. (That's why you have the drop cloth!) It's not good for an egg to have a broken shell, and it's not good for us to refuse to forgive our family and friends.
- Pass around some eggshells. The children will think of someone they need to ask forgiveness from or someone they need to forgive.
- Each child will break off a good sized piece of the shell and say, "Please help me forgive others when they do me wrong, and help me to be willing to ask for forgiveness."
- If you'd like, you can provide fine tip permanent markers so the kids can write "FORGIVE" on their eggshell. It will be a reminder for them to not just talk, talk, talk, but to forgive.
- Prayer will help make you strong enough to forgive, so pray often and seriously about those situations that need forgiveness.
- Let the children hear you pray for them to understand how important forgiveness is for them to grow into the people God wants them to be.

God Speaks:

Make allowance for each other's faults, and forgive anyone who offends you. Remember, the Lord forgave you, so you must forgive others. Colossians 3:13 (NLT)

Encouragement Prayers

Objective: To show how prayer can be a type of encouragement, especially if they let the person know he or she has been remembered in prayer.

Before You Begin...
1. What does "encouragement" mean to you?
2. Many times what people need most is encouragement.
3. They need encouragement:
    a. when they are afraid of what they have been asked to do
    b. when they are getting ready to try something new
    c. when they've had to talk to someone about a problem
    d. when they're going into a big game or have a major test
4. They may need encouragement when they know they need to ask someone to forgive them.

Prayer Time
- The children will name other times when people need encouragement.
- When do you need encouragement? This will naturally move into the kids sharing specific names of people who need encouragement, and that's good. That brings it to a more personal level.
- Write each name or situation where the kids can see them.
- Then, designate one child to pray for each need for encouragement.

Teachable Moments
When we pray for someone, that encourages her or him. God can be with them when we can't. But, it's also nice to remind people that they are being prayed for. You can do that through an email, Facebook, a phone call, a text or a written note. When you put your encouragement into action like that, your prayer becomes even more encouraging. Get out your phone and let the kids text someone right now and encourage them.

God Speaks:
So encourage each other and build each other up, just as you are already doing. 1 Thessalonians 5:11 (NLT)

Fiery Furnace Prayer

**Objective: To help kids understand that God's presence
is right there with them when they ask.**

Materials
- Bibles
- Copies of the footprints

Before You Begin...
1. Run copies of the footprints (on the next page) and use them to make footprint paths all over the room by laying these in a walking pattern.
2. Place a couple of Bibles in various places across the front of the room. Each footprint path should lead to one of the Bibles.

Teachable Moments
Since the Bible is God's words to us, we're going to use it to represent God's presence or God being with us. Instruct the children that if they or someone they are close to is going through a difficult time, they can come and place a hand on one of the Bibles.

Prayer Time
- Children will find a footprint path close to where they are sitting to follow to a Bible. When the child reaches a Bible, encourage him to lay a hand on the Bible and say, "God, I need you to walk with me through _____." Then, ask him to just stay there as others come to place their hands on the Bible also.
- Shadrach, Meshach, and Abednego had each other in the furnace, as well as God, and it is good to be surrounded by our friends in prayer.
  - o The kids at each Bible will keep one hand on the Bible and then place their other hand on the back of someone's who is standing with them as you pray together.
- Finish your prayer time by asking the children to repeat after you each of these phrases:

> **Dear God, (Dear God,)**
>
> **Because You have offered, (Because You have offered,)**
> **We ask that You make us free (We ask that You make us free)**
> **to walk with You (to walk with You)**
> **through anything! (through anything!)**
>
> **Amen. (Amen.)**

God Speaks:
If we are thrown into the blazing furnace, the God we serve is able to save us from it, and he will rescue us from your hand, O king. But even if he does not, we want you to know, O king, that we will not serve your gods or worship the image of gold you have set up. Daniel 3:17-18 (NIV)

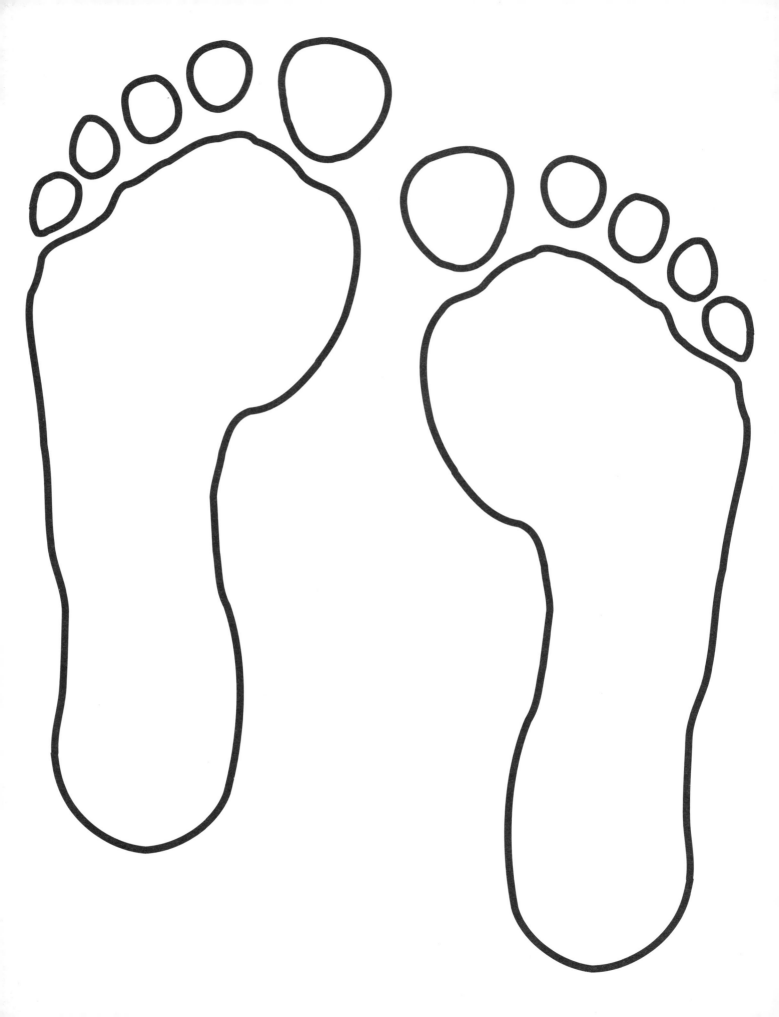

Five-Finger Prayer

Objective: To teach kids an easy prayer guide.

Teachable Moments

A prayer guide is right at the end of your arm. Hold your hand so your thumb is almost at your mouth and your pinkie is away from you. Use each finger as a reminder and prompt to pray for specific people.

Prayer Time

- **Thumb** - Your thumb is closest to your face. Pray for the people who are closest to you, like your family and friends

- **Index Finger** - People who teach you sometimes point their finger at you. (Shake your finger at someone.) Pray for your teachers at school, teachers at church, coaches, instructors, and for your pastors.

- **Middle Finger** - This is your tallest finger. It stands out above the others. Pray for your leaders, both in your country and in your church, who go out ahead of you.

- **Ring Finger** - Did you know that your ring finger is your weakest finger? Pray for people who are weak. This includes those who are sick, have lost a loved one, have been orphaned, are thinking about suicide, and are homeless. Can you name other people who are in a weak situation?

- **Pinkie Finger** - Your pinkie finger is the farthest one from your face. Pray for people who are far away in other parts of the world that they will come to know Jesus.

God Speaks:

Even there your hand will guide me, your right hand will hold me fast. Psalm 139:10 (NIV)

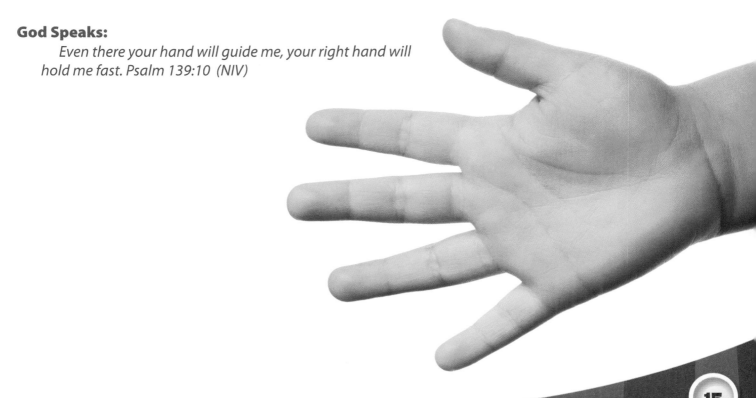

Fully Committed Prayer

Objective: To help kids understand what being full committed to God looks like.

Materials
- Crayons
- Paper person cut-outs

Teachable Moments

What does it mean to be fully committed to God? It means that you give God everything, every moment, every action, and every thought. When you're fully committed, you go to God for help with every decision. There is nothing in your life that doesn't involve Him. Wow! What a different life each of us would have if we could say that we are fully committed! Can you name some people of faith in the Bible who were fully committed?

Prayer Time
- Make a copy of the person cut-out on the next page, giving each child a cut-out and one crayon.
- Give them a few moments to evaluate where they are in being FULLY committed to the Lord. They can depict this by coloring in a portion of their paper person.
- If they feel they are just a little committed, then they should color in the feet or one leg—a small portion of the cut-out.
- If they feel they are FULLY committed, then they should color in the entire person. They will not be making faces and putting clothes on these cut-outs, only making a personal thermometer to measure how committed they are.

Pray together that God will show you how you can be more FULLY committed to Him.

God Speaks:

The eyes of the Lord search... those whose hearts are fully committed to him. 2 Chronicles 16:9 (NLT)

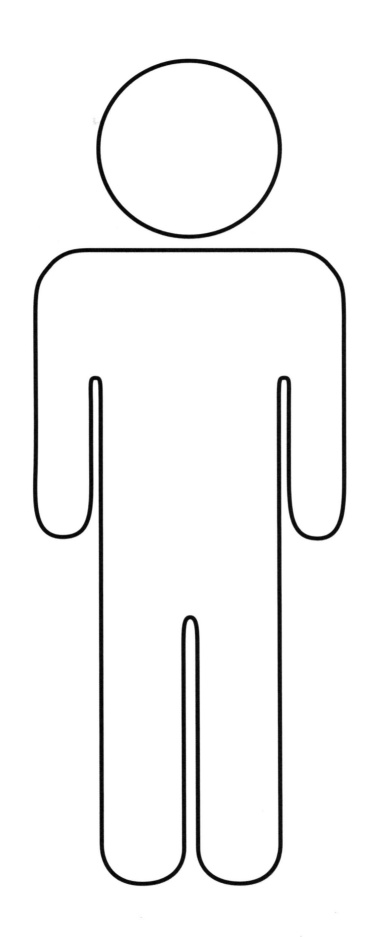

From the desk of: *tina!*

Get Started Young

When do you start teaching kids about prayer? Now! Wherever you are and however old they are. It is never too young. Indulge me for a little bit, because I'm going to share some of the joys of being a grandma.

Bowen and Kendall, our grand-twins, are now 21 months old. There's only one thing wrong with these two precious kids—they are 10 hours away. The last two times I visited them, when we got ready to ask the Lord's blessing on our meal, both of them folded their hands and occasionally said, "men" when Daddy said "Amen." Bowen would also signal that he thought it was time to get on with the eating by saying "men" in the middle of the prayer. We noticed that while the prayer was being spoken, Kendall would whisper her little words that no one yet understands. They are learning about prayer. What are they learning? They are learning that their family pauses to honor God together. As Joshua 24:15 (NLT) says, *"As for me and my family, we will serve the Lord."* They are learning that prayer is focusing on God and not on myself. They are learning that they can talk out loud and God, Whom they can't see, will hear.

The Bible is clear in Deuteronomy 6:6-7 (NKJV) that the spiritual development of the child is a responsibility of parents. There it tells us that children are to be taught "when we lie down and when we rise up." That's when children are at home. And prayer needs to be taught in the home on a daily basis for children to see it's a holy habit that is important to their everyday lives.

But even before BoBo and Sissy (as they call each other) started folding their hands and whispering at the table, they were taught about prayer (See the DEDICATION page for pictures of Bowen & Kendall praying). From their first night at home, Jarad has held them individually and spoken a blessing in their ear; it's the last thing he does before placing them in their cribs. Blessing your children (or anyone for that matter) is a way of praying over them…speaking God's truth to them. How wonderful for that to be the last thing they hear before going to sleep!

Consider all the things you teach your children. Most of them don't come out of a book. They come from modeling. How many times have you said or heard someone say something similar to, "I can't believe they did that at such a young age," or "I have no idea where that came from." If you look around, you'll realize they've been watching and listening to the people around them. They've seen it modeled, so they do it. Model a lifestyle of prayer and your children will grow to appreciate the gift they have—access to their Heavenly Father.

Go Team Prayer

Teachable Moment

Commiting to pray together as the body of Christ is very important. We find strength in knowing that others are surrounding us in prayer as we go through a difficult situation or just need daily guidance to make good choices. We are a family. We are a team!

Prayer Time

When there is one overwhelming need in your group, use this prayer activity.

- Maybe one of your class members was in a terrible car accident. Or, maybe the church is making a big decision about its future. Maybe your class is really concerned about a particular family and their needs. Whatever this one particular need, gather the children in a tight circle.

- There will be no specific order, but as each child prays about this concern, he or she will extend one hand to the center of the circle.

- When all have prayed, their hands should all be on top of one another--just like a team when it's getting ready to go out on the field for a big game.

- The leader will close with "Our confidence is in You, Lord," to which the children will all respond in a committed rally cry, "Aaaaaaa-men!"

God Speaks

Are any among you suffering? They should keep on praying about it. And those who have reason to be thankful should continually sing praises to the Lord. James 5:13 (NLT)

God's Timing Prayer

Objective: To learn how to trust God and His timing.

Materials
- Permanent markers
- Strips of old sheeting

Before You Begin...
Each child will need a piece of old sheeting 2"-3" wide and about 24" long. With a permanent marker, he will write "RIGHT NOW" in big letters on the strip of cloth.

Teachable Moments
Mary and Martha expected Jesus to come right away, but He waited three days before going to Lazarus. Remember what Mary said to Jesus when He arrived? She said, "Lord, if You had been here my brother would not have died." Mary couldn't think past her timing. She wanted Jesus to come NOW. Mary and Martha thought of God's power in their terms and their timing—NOW! In their minds, the only way they could see a miracle and God's power would be through healing Lazarus. But, our God is full of options that we can't imagine. Mary and Martha were bound by what they thought was the answer.

Prayer Time
- The kids will wrap the strip of cloth around their wrists several times. (They won't be able to do this by themselves, so encourage them to assist one another and offer adult help.)
- Is there anything that you've been praying about and you are sure the only answer is for God to do what you've asked right NOW? Are you a little disappointed that God hasn't answered the way you've prayed? God ALWAYS answers our prayers. He doesn't see your name pop up on caller ID and say, "Oh, I don't want to talk to them. I don't want to answer their question." He just knows what is best for us and what will cause us to give Him glory. Our lives should be about doing anything we can to bring God glory…and that means trusting Him and His timing.
- The kids will pray that they can trust God's timing and be free from thinking they have to have the answer NOW.
- Instead of saying "amen," the kids will pull their hands apart to unwind the strips of cloth and say, "Come forth!" God wants us to be free to trust Him and His timing.

God Speaks:
As the heavens are higher than the earth, so are my ways higher than your ways and my thoughts than your thoughts. Isaiah 55:9 (NIV)

Grab It Prayer

Objective: To learn how to be free from all kinds of things—free in Christ.

Materials
- Pencils
- Scrap paper
- Toy grabbers*
- Trash can

Before You Begin...
1. What do you need to be free of?
2. Do you need to ask God to change your life in a drastic way? Do you need to be set free from the sins that you've gotten yourself into? Do you need to come back to the God who created you?
3. Have you let your mouth say things that it shouldn't say? Do you need to be set free from a filthy mouth?
4. Have you been bullying other kids? Do you need to be set free from having to feel like you're "big and bad"?
5. Are you too comfortable with telling little lies? Do you need to be set free from lying?
6. Are you full of anger at your parents? Do you need to be set free from your awful anger?

Teachable Moments
We can become a prisoner to all kinds of things, but God wants us to be free in Him. We need to get free of the wrong things that are in our lives, so people can see Jesus in us. Write on the paper something that GRABS HOLD of your life…something that you keep doing even though you know it displeases God. What is it that you have a hard time shaking? No matter what you write on the paper, God has the power to free you from it, if that's what your heart wants.

Prayer Time
- Give the kids the opportunity to pray a silent prayer about what they wrote on their paper.
- When they are done, they will grab hold of their piece of paper with a grabber. With the grabber holding the paper, carry it to the trash can and dispose of it.
- As each kid releases his prayer paper into the trashcan, he will say, "God gives me freedom from sin!"
- Close in a group prayer, asking God to free each person from the things that shouldn't be in his life. Express the desire to live lives that show Jesus to the world.

God Speaks:
So if the Son sets you free, you will be free indeed. John 8:36 (NIV)

*Grabbers are little toys that have a trigger at one end of a handle to control the "pinchers" (or the mouth of an animal) at the other end, so you can open and close it. You can purchase these through novelty sites (like orientaltrading.com) where they are referred to as "Grabbers."

From the desk of: *tina!*

Growing Through Prayer

As a child, every day closed for me with one of my parents sitting on the side of my bed, the covers pulled up under my chin, and me muttering…

Now I lay me down to sleep.
I pray the Lord my soul to keep.
IF I SHOULD DIE BEFORE I WAKE,
I pray the Lord my soul to take.

Night after night after night after night, that third line sent chills through me. Most certainly, some frightened adult had written that prayer poem out of the desire of his heart, but it lived on to torture children all over the world, right before they went down for a restful night's sleep. After a while, I just let the words tumble out of my mouth and tried not to think about what any of it actually meant. And, this is one of the prominent ways we teach children to pray—a rhyme repeated over and over, with no real meaning to the child.

Another way we teach children to pray is nothing short of a Santa's wish list. We ask children to share their requests, which is another way of saying, "Let's tell God what you want Him to do for you." They quickly rattle off a long "To Do" list of relatives and friends who are sick and pets that are missing. Then, we acknowledge God answers prayer only if God does it the way we've suggested. This may come as a surprise, but God really answers every prayer. His answers are of such a wide variety we can't even imagine the possibilities. It's an everyday occurrence, though, to hear someone say, "God still answers prayer," when what they mean is, "God answered in the way I wanted Him to!"

Is this how we should teach our children to pray? Scary prayers? Prayers that fall from their tongues without thought? Prayers that find themselves alongside nursery rhymes? Prayers that instruct God about what He's supposed to do for us? What would your best friend think if every time you spoke with her, you just repeated the same rhyme? She most certainly wouldn't be your friend for long if all you ever talked about was what you wanted her to do for you. Something needs to change in the way we teach our children to pray.

We're just downright good at getting ourselves into messes and then praying that God will get us out of them somehow. Instead of praying for deliverance from the mess, what if we started teaching our children to pray in the middle of the mess, not with their minds set on deliverance, but simply asking God to help them see how they can grow in His wisdom as they go through it? How about praying for the strength to make it through to the other side?

If you look back on your life and identify the times when you grew spiritually—those times when spiritual growth seemed to come in leaps and bounds—I imagine you would say the greatest growth was in times of struggle. During those times when there were more questions about life than there were answers, you felt God moving in your life in a tremendous way. That's when you saw miracles happen. That's when you found yourself resting in His presence. Through those times, spiritual truth became clearer. So, why do we shy away from that? Why do we pray that we never have to experience it? Why do we teach our children to pray safe prayers that if answered in the way they are prayed, would only keep them from searching for God's truth and His plan for their lives?

As a newlywed 34 years ago, I woke my husband up in the middle of the night to ask him a question, "Why do we need to pray if God already knows everything?" I was content to ask the question then roll over and go back to sleep. My husband, on the other hand, wrestled with the question the rest of the night. Over the years, we've come back to that conversation and it's been a growing time. So, why do we pray? It's about coming into His presence. It's about being part of a relationship that is alive and full of meaning. I've talked to a lot of children's workers, and they all shake their heads in unison when I talk about those times when we look up and see parents at the door. We put our words in high speed and quickly tell the kids to bow their heads and close their eyes so we can pray. While YOU have your head bowed, the kids are putting their jackets on and not at all thinking about spending time in the presence of God. That sure doesn't feel like leading the children to a relationship that is alive and full. The Lord deserves an apology.

One of the first things you can do to elevate the importance of prayer is change where it falls in your time with the kids. We open with a ceremonial prayer and then close haphazardly. The children know what to expect so their brains experience something similar to the sound that depicts the off-screen teacher on the Charlie Brown cartoons…blah-blah-blah-blah-blah. Think about the ways you experience a friend. You share a meal, together. You go to a game with rowdy fans, together. You sit with them in silence as they grieve the loss of a loved one. You sing karaoke with them. You sit quietly on a dock, waiting for a fish to bite. We need to teach our kids that there are an endless number of ways they can experience the presence of God through prayer.

Prayer is a spiritual discipline, and like other disciplines, it needs to be practiced and experienced on a regular basis in order to become something we can't imagine living without. So, our challenge is to give children an opportunity to experience the presence of God in different ways. They need to be shown how each time they engage in a conversation with God, it can be new and fresh. Prayer should be a time of evaluation, when each person makes a conscious effort to identify his or her spiritual condition and expose that before the Lord.

The best way to teach kids to pray is to help them understand there is no set place or position or time of day. Since God is omnipresent, and prayer is experiencing the presence of God, then anywhere, any time, any position is in fair territory.

The goal of this book is twofold. I hope it gets your creative juices flowing about how, when, and where you can lead kids in prayer. And, I want to give you permission to do it! Even if it may be a little out of your comfort zone at first, go ahead and embrace the experience. You may be surprised that as you lead the children, you will find prayer avenues you really connect with also.

Let's raise this generation of kids to feel at ease with prayer and know it as a real conversation, not just a rhyme or a give-me list. Let's raise them not to be afraid of going through any life situation, because God will be with them and teach them great spiritual truth on the journey.

Handle with Prayer

Objective: To help kids learn how to handle feelings with prayer.

Materials
- Bruised banana
- Ripe banana
- Supply of bananas

Before You Begin...
You will need a banana that is beautiful and ripe and you'll need one that has obvious bruises.

Teachable Moments
Show the bananas to the kids. What differences can you see when you look at these bananas? One is really bruised! How do you think it got so bruised?

To keep a banana from bruising, you have to treat it gently. When you get it at the grocery store, you put it in a bag by itself or on the very top of a bag of groceries. You don't set anything on top of it.

Have you ever had a bruise? Maybe you turned a corner too quickly and rammed your arm into the door. Or you were wrestling in the floor and hit your knee on the coffee table. Or, you were riding your bike and took a tumble...yeah, your bruises were everywhere! A bruise leaves a mark and it hurts. Those are physical bruises, and we can see physical bruises. But, there are also bruises on the inside that we can't see. How do your feelings get bruised? Does your spirit ever get bruised?

The kids will poke themselves in the arm (very discreetly) for each of the following times when they get their feelings bruised. If the kids have listed their own times, add those to this list.

Prayer Time
My feelings get bruised when...
- Someone calls me a name.
- Someone says that I'm not good enough.
- I don't get picked for a team.
- Mom or Dad yells at me.
- I'm not good at something.
- I forget my lines in front of an audience.
- Everyone yells at me for missing a play in the game.
- Give each kid a banana to hold with care.
    - You've heard it said that breakable (and bruisable) things should be "handled with care." When those times happen and our feelings are bruised, we can "handle them with prayer."
- Go back through the list and ask God to help the kids who get their feelings bruised at those times.

God Speaks:

Don't worry about anything; instead, pray about everything. Tell God what you need, and thank him for all he has done. Then you will experience God's peace, which exceeds anything we can understand. His peace will guard your hearts and minds as you live in Christ Jesus. Philippians 4:6-7 (NLT)

High and Lifted Up Prayer

Objective: To teach kids to lift God high through our praise.

Materials
- Crepe paper streamers
- Paint stir stick
- Scissors
- Tape

Teachable Moments

The kids will make very simple praise sticks by taping brightly colored crepe paper streamers to one end of a paint stir stick or dowel rod.

Can you imagine what it would be like to see God sitting on His throne? Isaiah got a glimpse of what it was like and he describes it in Isaiah 6:1. He says that God was "high and lifted up." Isn't that a wonderful thing to think about?

In our minds and our hearts, God should always be "high and lifted up." When you lift your chin and look to the sky, you can imagine the angels singing "high and lifted up." Everything we do should send a message to everyone around us that we want to lift God high. We do that with our praise, the way we live, our worship and prayer.

Prayer Time
- As the time of prayer begins, encourage the children to pray a one-sentence prayer of praise and worship.
- At the end of each sentence prayer, all the kids will raise their praise sticks high in the air and say, "May the Lord be high and lifted up!"
- Repeat with each child praying, followed by raising the praise sticks again and saying, "May the Lord be high and lifted up!"
- We honor God when we pray. He is high and lifted up by our prayers!

God Speaks:

In the year that King Uzziah died I saw also the Lord sitting upon a throne, high and lifted up, and his train filled the temple. Isaiah 6:1 (KJV)

Hurried Prayers

Objective: To help kids understand that God wants them to spend time talking to Him—not to rush.

Teachable Moments

There are lots of people in this room, but it would be nice to greet each one.

Set the timer for 30 seconds and challenge the children to greet every single person in the room before it buzzes. Once you give the signal to start, the kids must shake hands, say "good morning," and tell their name to each person they greet. Anyone who completes their greetings before the timer goes off should sit down. Everyone, including adults in the room, should participate.

Did you learn anything that you didn't already know about anyone? (Not really, because we were too hurried. There wasn't time.) Did anyone who greeted you make you feel really special? Why not? How did it make you feel to hurry through our greetings this way? How does this remind you of the way we pray sometimes? (We're told what to say; we get in a hurry; we only say what we have to say and get it over with.)

How do you think God feels when we rush through our prayer time? God doesn't want us to pray because someone else told us what to say. He doesn't want us to cram talking with Him into a designated amount of time. He wants us to talk to Him from the things that our heart is speaking.

When we hurry through being with someone so we can go somewhere else that person will probably not feel that we care much for him or her— wherever we're going or whatever we're going to do must be a lot more enjoyable and important. If all we give to God is hurried time, then God gets the message that He isn't special to us or worthy of our love and time.

Prayer Time

What's the condition of your heart? Are you sad? Excited? Worried? Take a deep breath; don't look at the clock, and just relax. Tell God the things that are on your mind and heart. Then listen to what He has to tell you. That's praying the way God wants you to talk with Him!

God Speaks:

Great is the Lord! He is most worthy of praise! No one can measure his greatness. Psalm 145:3 (NLT)

In Remembrance of Me Prayer

Objective: To use special religious symbols or other objects to help kids remember something special about God, or others who need prayer.

Materials
- A souvenir

Teachable Moments

There are words written on the altar table at the front of the worship area. Have any of you ever noticed what it says there? It says, "In remembrance of Me." Who are we supposed to remember? (Jesus)

Jesus shared with His disciples the ceremony of communion so that when we eat the bread we have something to help us remember His body that was broken for us. And, when we drink the juice, we have something to help us remember His blood that was spilled for us. The bread and the juice help us remember that Jesus died on the cross for each of us.

Then Jesus picked up a towel and a basin of water and washed the disciples' feet—to help us remember that He came to serve others, not to be served.

Show the children a souvenir that you brought back from a special vacation. Tell them what it helps you remember about that vacation. Then, ask the children to share with the kids around them about a keepsake or souvenir they have that reminds them of something they did or someone they love.

Prayer Time
- When you pray in remembrance, ask the children to take turns praying out loud, finishing this simple sentence: I want to remember _____.
- They will fill in the rest of the sentence with whatever they want to tell God they will remember about Him.
  - I want to remember that You died for me.
  - I want to remember that You love me more than anyone does.
  - I want to remember that You want me to serve others.
  - I want to remember that You like to hear me sing.
  - I want to remember that You want me to serve you 24/7.

Dear God,

We want to remember how wonderful it was that You sent Your Son for us. Each time we use a towel, or eat bread, or drink juice, or sing a praise song, we want to remember how awesome You are and how important You are in our lives. Thank You for doing for us what we couldn't do for ourselves.

And the children said…amen.

God Speaks:
Do this in remembrance of me. Luke 22:19 (NIV)

From the desk of:
tina!

In the Middle of the Night

I'd like to share with you a chapter of my life that greatly influenced the way I pray. On my 18th birthday I was diagnosed with crippling rheumatoid arthritis. It took hold of me in a quick and violent way. But, because I was young and otherwise healthy, pharmaceutical companies and research organizations often asked me to be part of their studies. This was one of those times.

I had consented to be a human guinea pig at Stanford University in a study they were doing in search of a cure for rheumatoid arthritis. Participants would go through six weeks of daily total lymphoid radiation treatments. There were a few obstacles: finding a place to live since we lived over four hours away, and dealing with excruciating pain because I would have to stop taking almost all of my other medications.

In a hotel room close to the university, Ray and I prepared for the ordeal that would start the next day. I was glad the room had a small partition separating the two single beds. Ray had been a rock with me through the long and emotional day and needed to get a good night's sleep. The partition provided enough sound barrier that he wasn't constantly being awakened by my tossing, moaning and crying. The uncertainty about what radiation treatment was truly like, the tiring day of travel, and the fact that my cortisone had been so drastically lowered made the night seem like a year to me.

I would take a pain pill, roll over and cry myself to sleep, doze for a few minutes and wake up, only to start the cycle over again. The short sleep seemed as though it could've been a couple of hours so I would take another pain pill. In reality, only a few minutes had passed. After seven pain pills, and no relief whatsoever, I realized the night was far from over.

I kept trying to think of something that would occupy my mind and distract me from the pain. My thoughts wandered to the people back home. Earlier that evening two, 24-hour prayer vigils had started on my behalf, in which someone was scheduled to be in the prayer room, petitioning for my situation—every hour of the day and night for 24 hours.

I knew at this absurd hour of the night there were people praying for me. Somehow I felt their companionship in those long, dark, painful hours. I couldn't stand it any longer, and I had to know how much time was left of nightfall, so I woke Ray. He stumbled for the light and said it was 3:00 A.M. Who was praying for me at a few minutes after 3:00 A.M.? I lay there and thought about this unknown person and thanked God for his or her devotion and petitions of love.

About a year later I was going through the momentos I had been given from that night, which included a schedule of who was praying at the vigil. Out of curiosity I wanted to know who it was that was praying at a little after 3:00 A.M. There was the name—John Jones—a dear friend and co-worker.

In a conversation with John some time later, the prayer vigil became a topic of discussion. John shared how much it meant to him to be able to pray for me. He went on to say that while he was at the church in the middle of the night, he had a strong desire to lie down on the floor, humbled before God, and poor out his heart in a way he had never done before. The thought of responding to this feeling scared him, because he was afraid someone might walk in on him, thinking him a big eccentric. He recalled experiencing the presence of God telling him that if he was serious, he could humble himself that way…"Get on the floor!" So, denying his personal fear of what someone might think, he dropped to the floor, his face in the carpet, and prayed for me.

It was with great joy that I was able to tell him how I felt a companionship at that hour and how it had given me strength and courage. It was like an episode out of the *Twilight Zone*. Love found a way to overcome time and space through humility and prayer.

In Their Shoes Prayers

Objective: To help kids learn how to pray better for people by picturing themselves in their situations.

Teachable Moments

There's a saying, "Don't judge a man until you've walked a mile in his shoes." That means we should never assume we can even start to understand how people feel or what they're going through until we've gone through the same thing ourselves.

You can pray for someone in a more knowledgeable way when you understand his or her situation a little better. Once you get a glimpse into someone's life and the things they're facing, you will naturally pray more diligently for them.

Prayer Time

- Although this may be difficult to do while your group of kids are together at church, you can encourage them to pray this way during the week.
- Find a pair of shoes that actually belong to the person you're praying for (like your mom or dad) and put those shoes on.
    - o Imagine what that person is going to be doing that day. Think about what may concern or worry him.
    - o Think about the things that she needs to celebrate.
    - o Why are you thankful for this person?
    - o Pray about all these things and place this person in God's care.
- If you can't stand in his shoes, then sit in his chair or a place where you would find him regularly.
    - o When you're praying for your pastor, go sit in the seat where he usually sits for worship service.
    - o When you're praying for your teacher, sit at your group circle where he/she usually sits.
    - o When you're praying for your coach, sit on the bench after practice is over and pray for him.
    - o When you're praying for your grandpa, sit in his stuffed rocker.

- Step into someone else's shoes and into their world and you'll find yourself praying for them in a new way.

God Speaks:

Look beneath the surface so you can judge correctly.
John 7:24 (NLT)

Incense Prayer

Objective: To teach kids how to offer sweet prayers to God.

Materials
- Candles
- Hand lotions
- Index cards
- Pencils
- Spices

Teachable Moments

Incense is mentioned many times in the Old Testament. In the tabernacle and the Temple, the priests burned this sweet-smelling substance. It was considered an offering to the Lord and the smell, along with the smoke, would rise as if going to heaven. The incense represented the prayers the people were sending to God. When His people talk with Him, their prayers are like a sweet smell.

Read Psalm 141:2 together. Provide some items that have specific scents, such as candles, spices, and hand lotions. Place these in various places around the room so the kids will not have to crowd when you give them time to smell each item.

Prayer Time
- On an index card, each kid will write down a sweet prayer God would love to hear. Then, choose one of the smells you think goes along with your sweet-smelling prayer. Lay your index card in front of the object with your matching smell.
- Now, light one of the sweet-smelling candles as you pray together. Let each child share the sweet prayer he or she wrote as an offering to God.

God Speaks

Accept my prayer as incense offered to you, and my upraised hands as an evening offering.
Psalm 141:2 (NLT)

Is God There?

Objective: To help kids build a relationship with God, even when they can't see Him.

Materials

- A guest the children know

Teachable Moments

The most important way to develop a relationship with God is through prayer. Prayer may be difficult for children at first, especially if they have trouble with the fact that they are talking to someone they can't see.

Ask the kids to name some things you can't see but you know they are real. There's wind, electricity, your brain, a baby inside her mother's belly.

Now, have the kids close their eyes and let them know that they need to keep them shut until you tell them to open them. Bring in a guest everyone knows. This could be a past teacher, a parent, or the pastor. This guest should carry on a conversation with the kids, asking questions and making comments in response. Now, the kids can open their eyes. Thank your guest.

Did you believe (guest's name) was real? Even though you couldn't see him when you were talking to him and he was talking to you, he was still right there. God is right here wanting to talk with us, even though we can't see Him. I know that's difficult to understand sometimes. That's where our faith comes in—we believe in God, even though we can't see Him.

Prayer Time

- We don't use the same sentences or words every time we talk with our parents or friends. But, we tend to use the same sentences and words when we pray. God just wants us to talk with Him—asking questions, listening for answers, and sharing what's on our hearts.
- As the leader, challenge yourself to get out of the prayer rut you may have gotten into. You are setting the prayer example for your kids. Don't be afraid to show emotion when you pray; that shows your kids the REAL relationship you have with God.

God Speaks

Now faith is being sure of what we hope for and certain of what we do not see. Hebrews 11:1 (NIV)

Jacket Prayers

Objective: To help kids understand the importance of a good Christian role model in their lives and how they can be one for others.

Materials
- Several cloaks or jackets

Teachable Moments

Does anyone know what a mentor is? A mentor is a wise and trusted teacher, someone who advises another person and supports him as he learns. In 2 Kings 2, we read about a wise prophet of God named Elijah. He had faithfully served God and did his very best to get rid of idol worship in Israel. Now, he was getting old, really old!

For quite some time he had mentored a young man named Elisha. Elisha listened to his wise teacher and watched everything Elijah did. Elisha took Elijah's advice and was honored by the time Elijah spent with him. God had chosen Elisha to be the next great prophet once Elijah was gone, so Elisha went everywhere with the old prophet.

One day, Elisha followed Elijah as he headed toward the Jordan River. When they reached the shore of the river, Elijah took off his cloak and smacked the water with it. When he did this, the waters parted so Elijah and Elisha walked to the other side on dry land. On the other side of the river, God sent a chariot and horses of fire that picked up Elijah and took him away…forever. Elijah would never return; he was now with God. Elisha looked down and there was Elijah's cloak. He picked it up and walked back toward the Jordan River. When he reached the river, he remembered what Elijah had done; he smacked the water with the cloak and the waters parted again so that Elisha could walk across. That's when Elisha realized that he was now the one the people would be looking toward as a prophet of God. I don't know if Elisha wore Elijah's coat, but I bet he kept it to remind him of his wonderful mentor.

Prayer Time

- Today we are going to use some jackets to help us pray. If your answer to any of the statements I make is "yes", and you would like to pray out loud about it, I'd like you to put on a jacket. The jacket probably won't fit, but Elijah's cloak probably didn't fit Elisha either. Wearing the jacket will remind you that God will give you a mentor—someone to watch, who will help you learn to be more like Him.

If you would like to pray:

- for a person to watch who loves God…put on a jacket.
- that you would act more like the person you already watch…put on a jacket.
- to be a person God is proud of when others watch you…put on a jacket.

You may have to do this several times, but it is important for the children to physically experience putting on Elijah's coat as they pray out loud.

God Speaks

Dear brothers and sisters, pattern your lives after mine, and learn from those who follow our example. Philippians 3:17 (NLT)

From the desk of: tina!

Jesus Prayed for You

John 17 tells us that right before going to the Garden of Gethsemane, Jesus prayed for His disciples—both the ones who were there with Him at that moment and the ones to come. At first glance, Jesus appears to be praying for the twelve He had chosen, but then He says in verse 20 (NLT), *I am praying not only for these disciples but also for all who will ever believe in me through their message.*

That's you and me! And it includes the children we lead to love Jesus the way we do. Isn't that incredible? In Jesus' most stressful moments, He thought of us and He remembered us to the Father. This should give each of us great encouragement. What He actually prayed is worthy of a good look. What did He desire for us? What was His vision for us?

He wanted His disciples, both then and through the ages to come, to receive the Word of the Father. There is great power in the Word of God. There is comfort. There is assurance. There is motivation. There is reprimand. There is direction. There are answers. The desire of His heart was for us to embrace the Word of God in every part of our lives. As a holy army that seeks the hearts of children for the Kingdom, this must be our prayer also…that the children who are in our care will grow to cherish every book, chapter, verse, and word of the Bible. Do you love the very words that God has written to you? Have you communicated in a passionate way how much you treasure the Word of God? Jesus prayed for you to love it! And He wants you to teach kids to love it also.

The longing of Jesus' heart was made clear as He prayed that we would be united through the power of His love. His prayer was that we would be protected from the boundaries that keep us from loving one another…really loving one another…that those walls would disappear and we would become family in its truest form.

Jesus didn't pray for us to be nice to one another or to know each other's names. It goes way beyond that. His desire? That without reservation we would lay down our lives for one another, because we wouldn't think of doing anything less for our family.

Unity doesn't come easily. It requires digging deep into the soul and throwing out the dirt that keeps us from seeing the treasure of relationships. Jesus wants that for you. He wants that for your kids. It starts with the way you love them.

Do you know your kids? Do you love them despite the dirty clothes they're wearing or the way they always grab for food? Do you love them when you find their language difficult to tolerate? Do you love them…really love them…as much as Jesus loves them?

Jesus prayed that you would be more than happy. He prayed that you would know the joy of the Lord. In this Scripture passage, Jesus acknowledges that we will be in the world, but He also knows we can still be filled with His joy. He wants that for you. He wants that for your kids! Be a living example for your kids of a life drenched in joy.

You were on His mind. Maybe He closed His eyes and saw your face flash in the darkness as He prayed right before going to the Garden of Gethsemane. You are still on His mind as He sits at the right hand of God, interceding for you. Be encouraged. He sees your efforts and He sees your heart. He is still praying for you and applauding every humble effort you make to impact the life of a child for His Kingdom.

Lay Down Your Treasure

Objective: To help kids understand what their most precious treasure should be—Jesus.

Materials
- Art paper
- Markers
- Packing tape
- Self-standing wooden cross

Before You Begin...

Construct a self-standing wooden cross out of two 4" x 4" posts. Ask one of the retired guys in your church who loves to play around with his power tools to put this together. He'll fix you up.

Give each kid a half-sheet of art paper. What is your most treasured possession? What would you be most upset about if it was destroyed or stolen? What would make you cry if it were suddenly taken from you? Draw a picture of the one thing you treasure more than anything else.

Teachable Moments

When Jesus left heaven and came to earth, He gave up His most treasured possession. Can you imagine leaving heaven to do anything? No place gets better than heaven! But Jesus left heaven to give Himself as a payment for our sins. What Jesus gave was bigger than anything we treasure.

Mark 12:41-44 tells us about a woman who gave her last two coins. She gave everything she had. Another woman in Mark 14:3-9 poured expensive perfume on Jesus. She gave an expensive, precious, personal treasure. But Jesus' gift to all of us was bigger than either of these gifts.

Now, look at the picture you have drawn. Jesus' gift is even bigger than the treasure you have drawn.

Prayer Time
- The kids will take their picture to the cross and attach it somewhere, using a loop of packing tape or duct tape. As each child places her treasure at the cross, encourage her to pray a simple prayer, "I give you my treasure. Help me not to get caught up in the things I have, because I want You to always be my most precious treasure."

God Speaks

For where your treasure is, there your heart will be also.
Luke 12:34 (NIV)

Left Hand, Right Hand Prayer

Objective: To use kids' hands to help them think about choices they make and communicate openly with God.

Teachable Moments

Left hand, right hand is a good way to pray, where the kids make a choice between two things. They signify their choice by what they do with their hands. The left hand represents one choice, while the right hand represents another.

Each time you teach a Bible story, the kids should find themselves in that story, making a choice as to how their life should be different according to what they just learned.

You can use the left hand, right hand prayer with the story of the 12 spies who went into the Promised Land. All 12 witnessed the same things while in the land, but they perceived those things differently because of their relationship with God. Joshua and Caleb trusted God and wanted to take the land that God brought them to. The other 10 men were afraid of what they saw and lacked the faith to see the possibilities God was giving them.

Prayer Time

- Hold out your hands. Let's say that your left hand represents the way Caleb and Joshua lived. And let's have your right hand represent how the 10 spies lived. (Review with the children which hand is which…left hand, right hand.) Now, let's close our eyes. Place either the right hand or the left hand in your lap according to which is right with the story.
- If you find the bad side of things, put your right hand in your lap (10 spies). If you have positive things to say, put your left hand in your lap (Caleb and Joshua).
- If your faith in God is weak, put your right hand in your lap (10 spies). If your faith in God is strong, put your left hand in your lap (Caleb and Joshua).
- If you talk people out of doing what the Lord wants, put your right hand in your lap (10 spies). If you encourage your friends to follow the Lord, put your left hand in your lap (Caleb and Joshua).

When our hands are flat against our laps, they can't hold anything. When our hands are turned upward, they can be filled.

- If you want to be the first person to speak God's words into someone else's life, turn your hands so they can be filled.
- If you are anxious to have a stronger faith in God like Caleb and Joshua, turn your hands so they can be filled.
- If you want to encourage the people around you to follow God, then turn your hands so they can be filled.
  Amen.

Even though this isn't the traditional way we conduct prayer, the children are able to communicate the desires of their hearts…and isn't that what prayer is all about!

God Speaks

I will praise you as long as I live, lifting up my hands to you in prayer. Psalm 63:4 (NLT)

Loosen the Grip

Objective: To teach kids to hold possessions lightly so they can hold tightly to God.

Materials
- 2 hard cover books (similar)
- Pencils
- Pieces of paper

Before You Begin...
1. Get someone to help you prepare the books.
2. Each person will hold a book and face one another. You are going to weave the books together. With the books laying flat in your hands, lay one back cover into the other book, overlapping them about halfway to the bookbinding. One person will drop a few pages and then the other person will drop a few pages. Back and forth, back and forth, alternating the pages that are dropped.
3. Continue doing this until all the pages have been woven together.

Teachable Moments
Choose two kids to participate in this demonstration. Facing one another, each kid will grab hold of the binding of a book. At the signal, they will try to pull the books apart. They won't be able to do it. Books like this have been fastened to the back of a pick-up truck, which wasn't able to pull them apart!

When you're consumed with greed, no matter what comes along, you won't let go of your possessions—they are too important to you. They are so important to you that it's almost impossible to get you to let go of anything you believe is "yours." These books remind us of people who are greedy and won't let go of their "stuff."

Prayer Time
- Encourage each child to think of one thing that is super important to him or her. Then, provide each child with a small piece of paper to write it on. After the kids have that "one thing" written on their paper, they will put it in one hand and clench their hand tightly around it.
- Maybe you're holding on to something you own too tightly. God does not want us to hold tightly to the "things" that belong to this world...our stuff. If you need to loosen your grip on the "thing" that is super important to you, as you pray, open your hand and let go of what you are holding on to so tightly.
- With our hands open, let's pray right now that we can all let go of whatever it is we're holding on to tightly. Let's pray that we will let go of any desires we have to be greedy. And, let's pray that we can learn how to use the things we have to help others and to show them God's love. Hold your hands out and open them. Let go of whatever you are holding on to too tightly.

God Speaks
Then he said, "Beware! Don't be greedy for what you don't have. Real life is not measured by how much we own." Luke 12:15 (NLT)

Megaphone Prayer

Objective: To encourage kids to share the Good News of Jesus with those who don't know Him.

Materials
- Mailing labels
- Markers
- Megaphones

Before You Begin...
1. The kids can make megaphones or give each child a small megaphone purchased through a novelty store/website such as orientaltrading.com.
2. If making a megaphone, cut a circle of stiff paper that has a radius the length you want your megaphone. Mark the center. Cut a piece out of the circle that would be about two-thirds of the pie (by cutting into the center point in two places).
3. Also, each child will need a mailing label that still has the backing on it.

Teachable Moments
Who uses a megaphone? (A cheerleader. A coach. A person giving instructions to a large group.) When you use a megaphone, it's because you want to make sure your message is heard clearly. A megaphone focuses the sound and makes it louder.

Each child will write, on the label, the name of one friend or family member he or she would like to tell about Jesus. You want your message to be loud and heard clearly. Even though you probably wouldn't scream the Good News of Jesus at people with a megaphone, you don't want the message to get lost in all the other sounds that are going on around you.

Prayer Time
- Peel the backing off the mailing label and adhere it to the inside of the megaphone securely.
- The kids will take turns praying for the person they wrote on their label (which is now on the inner wall of their megaphone). They can hold the megaphone up to their mouth as they pray...how cool! Encourage them to pray that God will give them the personal courage and the right words to say when the opportunity comes to talk to their person about Jesus.

God Speaks
I do everything to spread the Good News and share in its blessings. 1 Corinthians 9:23 (NLT)

Mercy Prayer

Objective: To remind those who have accepted Jesus of that gift, and to encourage those who haven't to think about their need of God's mercy.

Materials
- Markers

Before You Begin...

Give each child a marker so he or she can write the letters of the word "MERCY"—one letter on the pad of each finger/thumb on one hand. The letters of MERCY will help them as they pray. If they have accepted Jesus as their personal Savior, this is an appropriate prayer to remind them of that wonderful gift. If they have not made that decision, they can use this prayer to do just that. For other children: encourage them to think about their need for God's mercy.

Teachable Moments

Review why each letter in this prayer is important and what it represents.

M – Mercy that gives me...
(His mercy is for YOU, not just for other people.)

E – Eternity through the...
(When we accept God's gift of mercy, He gives us a forever future, an eternal future, with Him.)

R – Resurrection of...
(Jesus' death was different, because He was the only one Who didn't stay dead. God is more powerful than even death.)

C – Christ Jesus...
(He stepped up and willingly became the One who received all the punishment that should have been ours.)

Y – Your Son...
(God gave His Son, the one dearest and closest to Him. It wasn't just anybody who died for you and me; it was the Son of God!

Prayer Time

Dear God, Thank You for Your ...
- Mercy that gives me
- Eternity through the
- Resurrection of
- Christ Jesus
- Your Son.

God Speaks

Answer me when I call to you, O God who declares me innocent. Free me from my troubles. Have mercy on me and hear my prayer. Psalm 4:1(NLT)

Not-So-Independent Prayer

Objective: To realize that we all need help at some time in our lives, and God wants to help us at all times, if we just ask.

Materials
- Large piece of paper
- Marker

Before You Begin...
Make two columns on a large piece of paper. The heading on one column will be "By Myself" and the heading of the other column will be "Need Someone's Help."

Teachable Moments
Encourage the kids to list things they can do by themselves and then list things that they need help from someone else in order to do. They are proud of their independence and sometimes resist admitting there are things they need help with. So, as the leader, tell several things that you have to ask for help with.

There are times in our lives when we think we don't need God's help—maybe we think we have just a little problem and we're sure we can figure it out on our own. Or maybe it's a new project we want to try. Do we really want to do it on our own? God promises to be with us, to go with us through everything in our lives. He knows better than you or anyone else how to work through problems and how to succeed at the projects we attempt. He knows what's good for us and what we should run away from. It's always wise to seek God's help, even when we think we can do it by ourselves.

Each student will choose one of the things he listed in the "By Myself" column and one thing she listed in the "Need Someone's Help" column. Today they will focus on those two things.

Prayer Time
- Guide the kids to pray that they will...
    - welcome God even when they think they can make it on their own,
    - and that they will immediately invite Him to help them when something is overwhelming.
- They can fill in the blanks in the sentences below. (Teach them the motions that go along with "welcome" and "invite." This gives a physical dimension to the prayer that will help the kids remember).

Dear God, I welcome You to help me, even when I think I can _____ on my own. (welcome: make a motion like you are opening a door)

Dear God, I invite You to help me when I don't know how to _____. (invite: make a motion for someone to join you)

God Speaks
Seek his will in all you do, and he will show you which path to take. Proverbs 3:6 (NLT)

Obstacles Prayer

Objective: To help kids trust God and ask for His help in prayer as they face difficult times.

Materials
- Ballpoint pens
- Tongue depressor sticks

Teachable Moments

At the end of the journey when Paul was being taken as a prisoner to Rome, the ship dropped anchor in a place the captain wasn't familiar with, because the storm was tearing the boat apart. An angel of God told Paul how to save the crew and other prisoners. At Paul's signal, everyone would swim for shore. The ship was falling apart and some of the men who couldn't swim grabbed a piece of wood from the boat to float their way to shore.

Prayer is one of the main ways God gives us to be survivors through the difficult times. It's one of the resources we have available to us. We're going to use a piece of wood that reminds us of something the prisoners grabbed to stay afloat during their crazy situation.

- Give each child a tongue depressor stick (sometimes called jumbo craft sticks) and a ballpoint pen. (Pencil will not show up and markers bleed.)

- Each child will write down an obstacle he or she is facing right now. It may be something small or it could be something huge. It could be getting over the fear of water while taking a swimming class or a mom and dad having problems getting along.

- **Ask:** *What is your rough place? What are you having a difficult time handling or getting around right now? Write that on the tongue depressor stick.*

- Everyone on the ship grabbed hold of pieces of the boat. Let this tongue depressor stick remind you of a piece of the boat. It is going to be your stick to hold on to—the prayer to get you through your difficult time.

Prayer Time

- We all have difficult times, Lord. We know that. We know that You want us to be survivors. So, right now we want to bring You our obstacle and ask for Your help in getting through it. Please help us with _____.

- (Ask the kids to say altogether what they have written on their tongue depressors.) We don't want to bargain with You, or quit, or run away, or panic. We want to be survivors with Your help. Amen.

God Speaks

I have told you these things, so that in me you may have peace. In this world you will have trouble. But take heart! I have overcome the world. John 16:33 (NIV)

Palm Branch Prayer

**Objective: To teach kids that we can pray and just tell God
what we appreciate about Him. No asking. No complaining. Just praising!**

Materials
- Dark markers
- Green construction paper
- Green poster board
- Glue
- Scissors

Before You Begin...
1. If you have access to an Accucut™ machine (schools are usually willing to let you use theirs for special projects), then use the hand die-cut to make 7 green construction paper hands for each child. If you can't use an Accucut™, draw around their hands, or let them cut leaves from green paper.

2. Encourage your kids to write on the handprint what they would yell at Jesus if they were along the side of the road when He entered Jerusalem. Make it simple…remember, it's something you would want Him to hear through the crowd. Encourage the kids to offer praises to Jesus because of who He is and not so much for what He has done for them or provided for them. Collect these.

3. Tape each hand onto a piece of green poster board to make a gigantic palm leaf. Make sure the praise can be read on the hand. Cut around the edges, so the handprints make the edges of the leaf. Then, post these giant palms where they can be seen by your kids and others who are passing by. These giant palms will encourage others to stop and praise God.

Prayer Time
- Isn't it great when people say something really nice to you…and that's all they wanted to say? They didn't want anything. They didn't want to complain. They just wanted to tell you something they appreciate about you or point out something you did that was good.

- We can pray and just tell God what we appreciate about Him. No asking. No complaining. Just praising!

- As you pray, the kids will pray from the praise they wrote on their hand palm. After each prayer, all the children will respond with "Hosanna!" Then, instead of closing with "Amen," end with a unanimous and passionate "Hosanna!"

God Speaks
The crowds that went ahead of him and those that followed shouted, "Hosanna to the Son of David! Blessed is he who comes in the name of the Lord! Hosanna in the highest!" Matthew 21:9 (NIV)

Palms Down, Palms Up

Objective: To let loose of things that get between us and God, and to receive what God wants to give us.

Prayer Time

- Go through the physical act of turning your hands palms down, in a dumping motion. At this point, the children will pray about what they need to turn over to God.

- What is it that is consuming you and causing a weight on your spirit? This is a cleansing exercise… to get these things out of the way… release them and verbally acknowledge that you're giving them up.

  o Maybe it is disappointment over something that's happened.

  o It could be anger toward a friend, sibling, or coach.

  o Frustration, worry, hurt feelings, sadness, resentment are all things they should consider turning over to God.

- Now, you're ready to receive what God wants to give you. Turn your palms up. Go through each one of the situations that you dumped in the palms-down prayer and ask for God's help in receiving what He has in that situation. Identify the quality that you need to receive.

  o If they had prayed earlier about a disappointment over not being chosen for a position on the baseball team, now is the time to pray to receive God's joy over the opportunity to play.

  o If they turned over their anger at a sibling, now is the time to pray to receive God's special love for that sibling.

  o If they turned over hurt feelings at what someone said to them, then now is the time to pray that God will give them an attitude of restoration, to mend that relationship.

  o If they turned over sadness over the death of a grandparent, then now is the time to pray that they can receive God's strength to look to the future.

- The palms up prayer is not praying for anything but what God wants to give us to heal what we have turned over (palms down) to Him.

God Speaks

Restore us, oh Almighty God, make your face shine upon us, that we may be saved. Psalm 80:7 (NIV)

Pass the Blessing

Objective: To learn how to pass a blessing to others around us.

Prayer Time

- The children will stand in a circle with their palms together—praying hands.

- The leader will begin by wrapping his or her hands around the hands of the child to the right. As the leader holds the child's hands, he or she will say, "God cares very much about you (insert child's name)."

- That child will turn to the child on his or her right, wrap his or her hands around the "praying hands" of that child and pass on the blessing by inserting the name of the child being spoken to. When the blessing has been passed all the way around the circle, the leader can close in prayer.

God Speaks

And without question, the person who has the power to give a blessing is greater than the one who is blessed. Hebrews 7:7 (NLT)

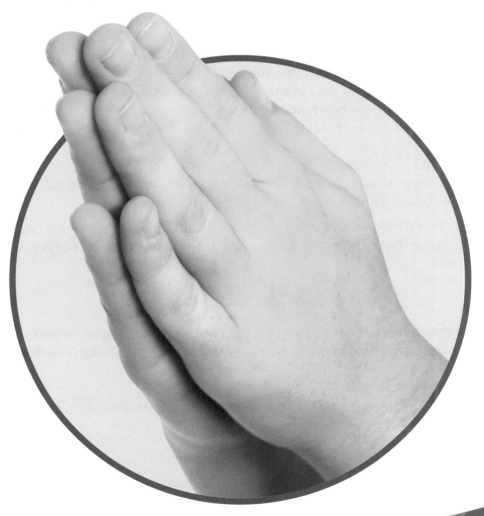

Piercing Prayers

Objective: To learn how prayer pierces sin's darkness and allows God's light to come in.

Materials
- Black poster board
- Nail
- Hammer
- Old magazines/newspaper
- Flashlight

Before You Begin...

1. Give each child a 5" square piece of black poster board. Kids will need an old magazine or a section of newspaper for padding. They will lay their piece of black poster board on the magazine and then poke some holes in the center of the square by holding a nail against it and tapping the head. Make 10-12 of these small punch holes.

2. Turn out the lights and one at a time let the kids put a flashlight up against their poster board card. Is the card able to keep the light behind it? (No, the light comes through the holes that are now in the card.)You can also show the difference between holding the flashlight up against a card that has no holes and one that does.

Teachable Moments

Sin is what happens when we allow Satan to spread his darkness in our lives. Hold up a piece of black poster board without the holes.

We live in darkness—we live in sin—when we follow Satan. Prayer does something about that though. Prayer pokes holes in Satan's darkness. It pierces the darkness and allows God's light to come in.

Prayer Time

- Pray with the children that their prayers will constantly poke holes in Satan's plans. Pray that God's light will always shine so bright in their lives that it will chase Satan's darkness away.

God Speaks

The light shines in the darkness, and the darkness has not understood it. John 1:5 (NIV)

Pit Prayers

Objective: To ask God to make something good out of bad situations.

Materials
- Paper
- Pencils
- Tub

Before You Begin...
1. You will need a large tub or a large piece of cardboard that you have made into a tub.
2. Paint the cardboard to look like stone or cover it with some of the corrugated stone-printed paper.

Teachable Moments

So many awful things happened to Joseph. It all started with his brothers throwing him into a cistern—kind of like a well where water was gathered from rainfall. Then, they sold him as a slave to some merchants who passed by going to Egypt. In Egypt he was thrown in prison for something he didn't do.

But, through all of it, Joseph remained faithful to God. He worked hard no matter his circumstances and lived a godly life. All those "pit"-iful things put him in a place where something wonderful could happen—the Pharaoh made him second in command of all of Egypt. When the drought came and his brothers came to Egypt for grain, Joseph was able to help them.

I love the verse in the Bible, Genesis 50:20 (NASB), where Joseph speaks to his brothers and says, "And as for you, you meant evil against me, but God meant it for good in order to bring about this present result, to preserve many people alive."

We have "pit"-iful situations sometimes too. There are bad things and difficult times in our lives—for adults and for kids.

Prayer Time
- Gather the children around the pit (the tub). They will draw or write about a difficult situation they are in the middle of right now.

- Encourage the children to put their paper in the pit when they are ready to do that. As they release their piece of paper, each child should pray, "God, I know that You can take my bad situation and make something good out of it."

God Speaks

And as for you, you meant evil against me, but God meant it for good in order to bring about this present result, to preserve many people alive. Genesis 50:20 (NASB)

Pizza Party Prayer

Objective: To change our focus: instead of making a list of orders for God, focus on praying that His presence will be real and obvious in our lives.

Materials
- Pizza

Before You Begin...
1. Call ahead and order a pizza to be delivered a few minutes earlier than you need it.
2. Pretend to call and order a pizza. (Which you ordered earlier.) Then, have a delivery person bring it in the door in just a few seconds. Wow! Now that's delivery! That's what I'm talking about…ask and you will receive!

Teachable Moments

How is the way we pray like ordering pizza? Now, how is it different?
1. Different pizza places have different guarantees. If the pizza isn't hot, they will give you a free pizza next time you order.
2. If the pizza isn't delivered at the time they tell you to expect it, then it's free.
3. Other places say, "If you buy a large pizza, we'll give you a free small pizza."

How are these guarantees and deals like the way we pray?
1. What is our attitude toward ordering pizza?
2. Do you ever feel like you're ordering something from God?
3. Have you bargained with God when you pray? Like, if You do this for me, then I'll do this for You, God.
4. What should our attitude toward prayer be?

Instead of making a list of orders for God, focus on praying that His presence will be real and obvious in your life. No matter what the pizza is like, it's the people you share it with that are really the best part. Now, enjoy that pepperoni pizza…or did you get sausage…or is it piled high with everything?

God Speaks
For everyone who exalts himself will be humbled, and he who humbles himself will be exalted.
Luke 14:11 (NIV)

Pounding Prayer

Objective: To learn how to handle conflict God's way through prayer.

Before You Begin...
YouTube download of "Bighorn Sheep Butting Heads"

Teachable Moments
What does conflict mean to you? Watch this YouTube video called "Bighorn Sheep Butting Heads." http://www.youtube.com/watch?v=hOYyrvsmRq4

These bighorn sheep were definitely in conflict. How did they handle it? They rammed each other in the head! Hopefully, we can deal with our conflict in a better way than butting heads. Sometimes when we're in the middle of a conflict, not seeing eye-to-eye with someone else, that's when a fight breaks out, and someone is likely to throw a fist or hurt someone else. Even if you don't take a swing, inside you're not thinking nice thoughts about the person you're in conflict with.

Ask everyone to pound one fist into the palm of the other. Really pound it! That represents the conflict. When you're in conflict, you get all tense and your fingers form a fist…whether or not you intend to hit anyone. That's one thing your body does when you're upset with someone. Now, open the hand that was making a fist. Lay your flat hand against the hand you just hit. That's better! When we open our hands, we're ready to set things aside, ready to receive, and ready to give.

Conflict happens when you want your way and you're being stubborn. It happens when someone insults you or calls you a name. It happens when you think you're better or stronger or smarter than the other person.

God has ways of helping us with our conflict, like when He helps us with our selfishness. Or, when He helps us keep our mouth shut or shows us how to walk away.

Prayer Time
The leader will say a line of the following prayer, and the kids will agree with that prayer by repeating it, adding their pounding fist or their flat hand to the end of the line as appropriate. When the children pound one fist into their other hand that represents their conflict. When they lay their flat hand in their other hand that represents how God wants them to handle their conflict with His help.

- When I want my way (pound fist), help me to stop being selfish (flat hand).
- When I want to come back with a smart remark (pound fist), help me to keep my mouth shut (flat hand).
- When I don't consider the feelings of others (pound fist), help me not to be stubborn (flat hand).
- When I think I'm better than someone else (pound fist), help me to remember that we're all the same in Your eyes (flat hand).
- When someone with the reputation as a troublemaker heads my way (pound fist), help me to walk away (flat hand). Amen.
- Be sure to include any other conflict prayers the kids have mentioned.

God Speaks
Do nothing out of selfish ambition or vain conceit, but in humility consider others better than yourselves. Philippians 2:3 (NIV)

Poverty Prayer

Objective: To become aware of people who live in poverty and learn how to pray for them.

Materials
- Video

Before You Begin...

1. You can find all kinds and lengths of videos online at sites like YouTube, on the topic of childhood poverty. Personally, I really appreciate the promotional videos put together by Operation Christmas Child. These videos depict a variety of cultures and give you a glimpse into the lives of children in all kinds of situations.

2. Once you've chosen a video on poverty, gather your children and turn down the lights. This should be a quiet, contemplative exercise.

Teachable Moments

When the video is over, ask the children to describe the part of the video that really stuck out to them. Do you remember the faces and situations of any of the children? Give each child an opportunity to describe the child they remember from the video.

Prayer Time

- Now, watch the video again. This time, when it comes to a place in the video that one of the kids has described as impacting them, push "pause."

- Identify which child spoke of this part of the video and ask her to lead a prayer for the specific child on the screen. Be ready for a life-changing time with your kids. This is powerful stuff!

God Speaks

You will always have the poor among you, but I will not be here with you much longer.
Matthew 26:11 (NLT)

Pray a Color

Objective: To use colors to thank God for all the colorful things
He has made for us to enjoy.

Materials
- Box of crayons

Teachable Moments

This is especially good with younger children. They are just learning to identify their colors and match things, so this is great mental exercise for them as well as leading them to pray.

Pull one crayon from a full box. Children will name everything they can think of that is that color.

Prayer Time
- With each identification, stop and say, "Thank You, God, for the orange _____." Smother God with thankfulness prayers of a particular color!

- This could easily become the prayer that parents use on a certain night of the week. Thursday is color prayer night! Only choose one color each time you use the color prayer, so that it stays specific.

God Speaks

Then I will praise God's name with singing, and I will honor him with thanksgiving. Psalm 69:30 (NLT)

Pray for Your Community

Objective: To pray for all who live and work in each child's community.

Materials
- Boxes
- Craft supplies
- Photos of community buildings

Before You Begin...
1. Take photos of buildings in your community the children are familiar with. Each building should represent a group of people. Some buildings you'll want to include are: hospital, police station, nursing home, jail, fire station, school administration building, orphanage, schools (especially any that are for special circumstances), rescue mission, family shelter, Social Security office, vocational rehabilitation, and/or Social Services office.
2. Provide the kids with a variety of boxes and craft materials. In small groups, they will work on their box to make it look like one of the community buildings you have shown them.

Teachable Moments
Place the boxes around the room. Each one of these buildings have people in them who need to be supported and surrounded in prayer. Some need strength and wisdom to do their jobs, like the police officers and firemen. Some need tender hearts and great knowledge, like the doctors and nurses in the hospitals. Some need to change their lives, like those at the rescue mission and jail.

Go through the buildings you're making so the kids can express how the people there need prayer.

Prayer Time
- The kids will choose one of the boxes/buildings to go to during prayer. It can be the one they worked on or a different one.
- The kids around each building will pray for the people who inhabit that place. If you have a place to store these boxes/buildings, they would be a great resource to pull out occasionally for this group or other groups.

God Speaks
Whenever I pray, I make my requests for all of you with joy. Philippians 1:4 (NLT)

Pray for Your Pastor

Objective: To learn how to pray for our pastor—the spiritual leader of our church family.

Materials
- Clear tape
- Lined index cards
- Pencils
- Picture of your pastor

Teachable Moments

Moses was the main leader of the Israelite people. His responsibility was to lead the people according to what God told him to do. Our church has a leader also—our pastor. His responsibility is to lead the people of this congregation according to what God tells him to do, just like Moses was doing. Here's a picture of our pastor. Show the picture to the kids.

We need to pray for our pastor. We should pray that:
- He will preach God's Word.
- He will understand the Bible.
- He will listen to the Holy Spirit.
- He will be kept safe.
- He will stay healthy.
- He will get good rest when he goes to sleep at night.
- He will enjoy his time with his family.
- He will always speak with God's wisdom.

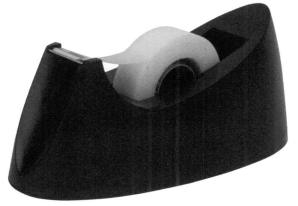

Prayer Time
- Give each child a lined index card and pencil. On their index card they will write a prayer for their pastor: "Dear God, please keep my pastor safe as he goes to visit people."
- Then, tape these cards together. Place the top of the second card against the bottom of the first card. Put tape across this seam. Then, place the top of the third card against the bottom of the second card BUT, this time you'll need to tape the seam on the underneath side. Go back and forth, taping on the top and then on the bottom. When all the cards are taped together, you can accordion fold the cards. When the pastor picks it up, the stream of cards will unfold all the way to the ground (if you have enough cards).
- Gather around the photo of the pastor that you brought in. The children will pray what they have written on the card they contributed. Each time a child prays, that child will reach forward and lay a hand on the picture. Let the pastor know that you are praying for him by presenting this unfolding card to him.

God Speaks

Pray also for me, that whenever I open my mouth, words may be given me so that I will fearlessly make known the mystery of the gospel, for which I am an ambassador in chains. Pray that I may declare it fearlessly, as I should. Ephesians 6:19-20 (NIV)

Pray like Moses

Objective: To learn to pray right away when problems come, and understand that God answers the prayers of those who love Him more than themselves.

Teachable Moments

When Korah rebelled against Moses' leadership, Numbers 16:4 tells us how Moses reacted. The first thing he did was "he fell face down on the ground." He wasn't playing dead. No, he fell to the ground and prayed. That's because Moses was a godly leader, and godly leaders go to the Lord in prayer as soon as there is a problem…not as a last resort when nothing else seems to work.

Moses knew he needed to pray and he needed to pray RIGHT NOW. In a desperate situation his first reaction was to pray. People who are following God's plan go to God. That's what godly people do. Moses didn't just bow his head and close his eyes. No, he threw himself on the ground and buried his head in his hands. He crumbled to the ground because this problem was so huge. Even his body was saying, "You are big, God. I am just Your lowly servant. I need Your help!"

Prayer Time

- The children will kneel on the floor, resting their bottoms back on their heels. Then they will lean forward with their head in their hands until their hands rest against the floor. This was probably the position that Moses was in when he prayed. Now, lead the children in prayer. Ask the kids to repeat each sentence; then, instruct them what to pray about in silence for a few moments.
- **Help us, Lord, to fill our minds with the right things. (repeat)** If there are things that shouldn't be in your mind—YUCK—ask God to take those out and fill your mind with the things that we read about in Philippians 4:8—things that are true, right, honorable, pure, lovely, excellent, and worthy of praise.
- **Thank You, Lord, for what I get to do in Your name. (repeat)** Think about the ways you can serve God and thank Him for those opportunities.
- **Help me focus on Your way and not worry about getting my own way. (repeat)** Do you spend more time thinking about what you want than about what God wants?
- **Help me to never be the reason that someone else sins. (repeat)** Pray that God will help you influence other kids to be more like Him. **Amen.**

God Speaks

When Moses heard this, he fell facedown. Numbers 16:4 (NIV)

Prayer Against Temptation

Objective: To learn to pray for ourselves and others when temptation comes—just as Jesus did.

Teachable Moments

When Jesus went to the wilderness for 40 days, Satan met Him there with all kinds of temptations. Jesus fasted during that time, so He had not had anything to eat for 40 days. How would you feel if you had gone 40 days without eating? (Weak, grumpy, sleepy) When you're hungry it's not a good time to deal with difficult situations, like the temptations Satan threw at Jesus.

But, Jesus had some weapons and ways of defending Himself against Satan's temptations. Jesus did not give in, even when Satan offered Him a way to have fresh bread for His empty belly. Jesus knew His stomach was not as important as staying true to God.

Jesus used the Word of God to beat Satan. He had the Scriptures in His heart and mind, so when Satan tempted Him, Jesus remembered the Scriptures for strength. And, Jesus just told Satan to get out of His sight—"Get behind Me, Satan." Jesus walked away from Satan's yapping.

Prayer Time

Ask the kids to repeat each line of this prayer.

Dear God,
Thank You that Jesus beat Satan's temptations.
Help me to do the same.
Help me not to compromise.
Help me to remember scriptures that will make me strong.
Help me to feel okay about walking away when I need to.
Help me to know when Satan is being sneaky.
Amen.

Now, let's pray this same prayer for each other. The Bible tells us to cover each other in prayer, and beating temptation is something we definitely need to pray about for our friends. Choose someone in this room you will pray for and say that name in place of "me."

Dear God,
Thank You that Jesus beat Satan's temptations.
Help _____ to do the same.
Help _____ not to compromise.
Help _____ to remember scriptures that will make them strong.
Help _____ to feel okay about leaving when they need to.
Help _____ know when Satan is being sneaky.
Amen.

God Speaks

Keep watch and pray, so that you will not give in to temptation. Matthew 26:41 (NLT)

Prayer Calendar

Day 1 - Pray for children who are in the hospital.

Day 2 - Pray for the leaders of our country.

Day 3 - Pray for the soldiers who fight for our freedom.

Day 4 - Pray to poke holes in Satan's power.

Day 5 - Pray for your mother.

Day 6 - Pray for your father.

Day 7 - Pray for your brothers and sisters.

Day 8 - Thank God for three special people in your life.

Day 9 - If you heard an ambulance siren today, pray for those people.

Day 10 - Pray for your teacher.

Day 11 - Pray that you will find a way to serve someone today.

Day 12 - Pray for your best friend.

Day 13 - Pray for the bully at school.

Day 14 - Pray for a friend who doesn't know Jesus.

Day 15 - Pray for your pastor.

Day 16 - Thank God for something that begins with every letter of the alphabet.

Day 17 - Pray about something that scares you.

Day 18 - Pray for someone who is sad.

Day 19 - Pray for your grandparents.

Day 20 - Pray for children who are hungry.

Day 21 - Pray for someone who has cancer.

Day 22 - Pray for doctors and nurses.

Day 23 - Pray for the people in jail.

Day 24 - Pray for your Sunday school teacher.

Day 25 - Pray for the kids at church.

Day 26 - Pray for older people who are hungry.

Day 27 - Pray that you will know God's plan for your life.

Day 28 - Pray for those working on cures for terrible diseases.

Day 29 - Pray that you will have courage to speak for God.

Day 30 - Pray for someone who is worried.

Day 31 - Pray for patience.

Prayer Eggs

Objective: To learn how to pray in God's will, not our own—just as Jesus did.

Materials
- Colorful lunch bags
- Copies of prayer slips
- Pencils
- Plastic eggs

Teachable Moments

When Jesus was in the Garden of Gethsemane, He poured out His heart to His Father in heaven. How awful it must have been to know He was going to be nailed to a cross and killed. But still, Jesus prayed and offered Himself to God's will.

Give each child a copy of the prayer strips and six plastic eggs. They will cut their strips apart and roll them around a pencil to make it easier for them to stay inside a plastic egg. Provide colorful lunch bags for the kids to put their prayer eggs in.

Each day, pull out an egg and read the prayer on the slip. This is only a starter prayer. Each prayer has something to do with one of the stories that occurred during Holy Week. You can put the prayer strip back in your egg and return it to your bag after you've prayed, because these prayer eggs can be used over and over. The prayer slips will never get old.

Prayer Time
- Dear Father, I don't want to act like I am ashamed to be one of Your followers. Help me to not be afraid when others ask me about You.
- Dear Father, I want to give with a cheerful heart, and I want to give You everything. That's what You deserve.
- Dear Father, help me to bear fruit and be all that You created me to be. I want others to know more about You because of how I live and what I say.
- Dear Father, help me to love others as much as I love myself. No, Father, help me to love them more than I love myself. It will take Your strength to do that. Remind me when I'm being selfish, and when I need to think of others more.
- Dear Father, if I had a palm branch I would wave it and shout Hosanna. I want to celebrate Your gift to me every day of my life. Hosanna to my King!
- Dear Father, help me to remember what You did for me when You sent Your Son, Jesus, to die on the cross and rise from the grave. When I see or taste the bread and the juice, I will stop all my other thoughts and be thankful.

God Speaks

I am praying to you because I know you will answer, O God. Bend down and listen as I pray.
Psalm 17:6 (NLT)

Prayer Environments

**Objective: To encourage kids to pray in unusual places—
not the same place—all the time.**

Teachable Moments

- Research tells us that when we sit in the same place (every day or every week) doing the same thing, our brains take in less information than if we sat in different places doing that same thing. That's interesting, because it tells us a lot about how much we take in during a church service. If your church is anything like the church where I worship (and I know it is), everyone has a pew or a row that is "theirs." That's where you'll find them sitting every week. The pastor can take attendance after the service by visualizing where the empty seats were and who is always in that place. When you sit in a different place, your brain has to shift out of remote and take in the information from a new perspective. It has to do some work! That's why we sit in the same place every week—because our brains don't have to work as much when we do. You are subconsciously being lazy! Try it this next Sunday. Instead of sitting in the back right section, move to the front left section. You'll be amazed at what you notice and how much more engaged in worship you'll be. You'll also be surprised at how many new people you meet during the greeting time.
- The same is true for prayer. If a child (or an adult for that matter) prays in the same place every day, saying the same words every time, his or her brain goes into that remote setting and engages less and less each time. Simply changing where the child prays can make a world of difference. Here are some ideas to get you started.

Prayer Time

- Pray in a tree. Yes, climb a tree and pray from up there. Look out over the neighborhood and pray for the people and homes that you can see from there.
- Pray in a tent. If you don't have a tent (and sometimes it's more fun if you don't), make your own with a king-size sheet. String a piece of rope from two points in the backyard and then hang the sheet over it. Crawl in your tent to pray. You can also drape the sheet over a card table in the house and have an indoor tent.
- Pray at the zoo. When you're enjoying a day at the zoo, find a place away from the flow of people but where you can see some of the animals. Thank God for His incredible creativity. Or, at each cage as you walk through the zoo, simply say thanks to Him for creating that particular animal.
- Pray at a statue, memorial, or military cemetery. This would be a wonderful tradition to start for your Memorial Day festivities, but would be effective any day of the year. Go to a commemorative military site. Pray for those who are presently serving our country to preserve our freedoms and helping others to have the same. Pray for the mothers and fathers, sisters and brothers, husbands, wives and children who have said good-bye to loved ones.
- Pray at a construction site. If your church or another church in town is building a new building, go stand near the construction and pray for those who will come to know the Lord in this place. Pray for the safety of those working on the site. And, pray for the leadership who will guide the people who will worship there.

- Pray in candlelight. Of course, you want to set boundaries and stress safety, but candlelight has the same effect on children as it does on a harried housewife who's soaking in a tub—a beautiful calming influence on the spirit. Praying by candlelight can be a very contemplative time for a child as well as a time when he or she can refocus after a stressful event.
- Pray in the garage. Here they can ask God to protect their family wherever they go, and to help them share His love with the people they meet in their travels.
- Pray at the farmers' market. Walk the rows and take note of all the beautiful fruits and vegetables the farmers have grown. Name those things individually, and thank God for each one. Isn't it amazing how many different foods God provides for us!
- Pray in the sandbox. Encourage the children to pray out loud as they move their hands around in the sand. Many children need a little physical stimulation to kick-start their brains, and this is just the ticket.
- Pray at the park. Take a walk through the park, go across the covered bridge, and throw a rock in the pond. Then, sit under a tree (or another spot that appeals to the child) to pray.
- Pray in a crawl-through tunnel. Those expanding tunnels are favorites of preschoolers. Kids love to crawl in with a book or just to hide from everyone. Now, it can be a prayer place too.

God Speaks

O my God, may your eyes be open and your ears attentive to all the prayers made to you in this place.
2 Chronicles 6:40 (NLT)

Prayer for Martyrs

Objective: To learn to pray for our brothers and sisters who do not enjoy the freedom to worship when and where they want to...like we do.

Materials
- Downloaded video

Before You Begin...
1. Do a Google search for the International Day of Prayer for the Persecuted or Voice of the Martyrs. There you should find videos that are 3-5 minutes in length that can be downloaded directly from the web site or off of YouTube. Make sure you preview the video in its entirety to confirm that it is appropriate for viewing by the age group you work with.
2. Together, watch a video about martyrs around the world. Give the children opportunity to react to what they have seen on the video. Rather than praying a blanket prayer around those who are under persecution, list specifics on the board that can be addressed through prayer (such as: different countries or cultures, protection for children, homes for those who have lost them, healing for the physical wounds they have received, courage to continue).

Prayer Time
- Recite Psalm 32:7 (NLT) together. *You are my hiding place; you protect me from trouble. You surround me with songs of victory.*
- Encourage the kids to pray for one specific thing you've listed on the board. After each child prays, the entire group will recite Psalm 32:7 (NLT) together as an affirmation that these persecuted people are in His hands. Make this a time of focused prayer where other needs are not addressed. Let's pray for our brothers and sisters who do not enjoy the freedom to worship when and where they want to...like we do.

God Speaks
You are my hiding place; you protect me from trouble. You surround me with songs of victory.
Psalm 32:7 (NLT)

Prayer Journaling

Spiritual growth through journaling

From the desk of: tina!

In recent years, school systems have put a huge emphasis on kids participating in regular journaling exercises. This is a great plus for the community of faith as we encourage kids to make spiritual journaling part of their personal disciplines. Just as individuals have preferences on hairstyles, clothing styles, the sports they play, and a plethora of other partialities they have, the actual form that journaling takes is specific to the person doing it.

First of all, let's just clarify what journaling, as a spiritual discipline, is. Journaling is when a person makes a record of something. That's where the similarities end, because from there, what is recorded, how it's recorded, and how much is recorded reflects the journaler's personality, spiritual maturity, and pathway strengths they prefer to use in processing information. Spiritual journaling is a way of carrying on a conversation with the Lord through the written word. The person journaling is just using a different medium that requires him to slow down and share thoughts that are more intentional and thought out.

The Bible is a collection of journaling. The Letters of Paul are full of descriptions of what is going on, his thoughts, and how he thinks certain issues should be resolved. David gives us insight into his personal spiritual journal through the Psalms—a poetic and musical journal. Matthew, Mark, Luke and John journal about many of the events they all witnessed, but each one gives us a different view, because they journal from a personal perspective. Even though some of it may seem to be "just the facts", the writer is choosing to share the God-experiences that specifically impressed his heart. Much of the Bible can be viewed as God's inspired Word being passed through the journals of these faithful followers.

Although I want to address intentionally equipping children to participate in spiritual journaling, the principles are just as relevant for teenagers and adults. So, if you're not journaling, before you encourage your kids to start, try out some of the ideas and approaches yourself. There is great value in journaling…not only for today, but for tomorrow, and for years down the road.

Spiritual journaling:

Helps to gain clarity. When you're having a difficult time understanding a concept or a scripture, writing down your random thoughts and then reviewing what you've written can be very insightful. It's like rotating a piece of a puzzle and when you hold it a certain way, you see where it fits all of a sudden. In times of confusion, journaling can be the instrument God uses to help you sort out what questions you actually need to ask. What's not making sense? Where do I get lost? It's prayer in a form we're not accustomed to.

Provides a safe place. There's no right or wrong in journaling. We have a big, mighty, powerful God who can handle our feelings; after all, He created them. The words penned there come from the heart. They may be very raw feelings, but they represent personal truth. It should be understood that journaling is private and it's something that adults should respect. You wouldn't tell someone their spoken prayer was wrong or needed correcting. Unless a child offers to share what he's written, the privacy of his journaling should be guarded. When I journaled along with a group of kids, we regularly held each other accountable. Each time we met, I also gave them a chance to share something they had journaled. At first, very few of them read from what they had written, but after awhile, they really enjoyed sharing entries, especially those that were evidence of how they had worked through a particular issue. They recognized how God was working in their lives and were very comfortable sharing those journal entries. Although it's different from what we're used to, they were sharing their answers to prayer.

Is a storehouse for years to come. One of the most valuable aspects of journaling is being able to look back. A journal is a record of spiritual growth; it's a record of conversations with God. Through the comments and perspectives shared there, years later a child will be able to celebrate and embrace the journey that God has taken him on. It's so rewarding to read about a spiritual struggle and then read months later how God has taken that incident and catapulted your spiritual understanding. That's why it's really important to date each entry in your journal. Without the dates penned in the journal, it's easy to miss out on recognizing where the spiritual journey has actually taken you.

Helps you meditate on God's Word. Psalms 1:2 (NIV) reminds us, *his delight is in the law of the Lord, and in His law he mediates day and night.* I think we all agree that it's a good thing to stop, get quiet, and just ponder what God's Word has to say…not so easy for kids many times though. Journaling can help kids, especially those who have a difficult time quieting their spirits, so they can meditate on Scripture. As they contemplate what to write, their minds are stretching and reaching for thoughts that are deeper than surface, off-the-cuff, "church-y" answers. In these moments, they pray through their written words, and are not "on-the-spot" to put their thoughts into words in the next ten seconds.

Fine-tunes our spiritual sight. When we look for God at work in the world around us, we see Him. When children know they will be journaling (talking with God), things that would normally go unnoticed are now God-sightings. Recognizing God moving in situations and lives that are near to the children is a source of spiritual strength and growth. Too often they don't tap into that source of strength simply because they don't notice. Journaling is a vehicle whereby kids pay attention and notice.

Articulate understanding and insights. Saying you understand something and being able to articulate it in the written word are two completely different things. Wrestling with words…just the right word…to say what it is that I'm actually thinking is mental exercise. But, as the words get rearranged and are hand-picked as a description, understanding of Scripture, expressing what is happening in your life, or something God is trying to teach a child comes into clearer view. Writing it down seems to help it make sense.

Is an expression of emotion. Journaling is a way for kids to vent their feelings to the Lord Himself. Understanding that what is written on the pages is between the child and God, and that God is big enough to handle any emotions that He created in us, can be a powerful tool for kids to access. Being able to express themselves, which may mean emotions they're not proud of or feel like others would disqualify, very often gives them a handle on the emotions that seem so out of control. Many emotions function purely as a way of saying, "I want and need to be heard" and praying, through journaling, can satisfy that need.

In school, kids are usually given a prompt and ten minutes to write whatever they think about that pertains to that prompt. It could be a sentence starter and the child goes on to write a short story from there. Or, it might be an old adage, like "A bird in the hand is worth two in the bush" that the child has to free-write about. A spiritual journal is similar in that you're writing whatever you can mine from your brain and your heart, but the focus is different. It's important that children keep in mind there is a purpose to their spiritual journaling and that purpose is to keep them on their spiritual journey with God.

I'd like to suggest a variety of forms that spiritual journaling can take. Just like anything else you do all the time, if it's always the same, you tend to lose interest. If you jog every day, changing your route can make a big difference on how quickly the time passes and what you notice on the way. If you like to read, there's something special about the first day that's warm enough for you to sit on the patio, enjoying the sunshine, while you crack open a new book. You can change up journaling by doing a few simple things.

- Provide different kinds of notebooks and writing utensils for the child to use. Kids who have a high word smart intelligence naturally love to play with words. But, one of the things that bring them additional joy when they write is being able to use a variety of papers and pens/markers/colored pencils. So, in August, when the stores are full of school supplies, purchase a few extra special writing implements that you can randomly present to the kids. You'll be pleasantly surprised at the boost this gives their journaling discipline.
- Let the kids decorate and personalize the cover of their journal. The traditional college composition books (you know, the black and white books full of lined pages for your essay questions that always made you hyperventilate?) make great journals for a couple of reasons. Right before school starts, you can usually purchase them for 25¢…that's a winner! And, the covers are sturdy enough that you can cover them with sticky paper or glue pictures on them without them disintegrating.

Encourage short-term types of journaling. Do a certain type of journaling for one month; then change. This gives the kids an opportunity to experiment with and find the type of journaling that is most beneficial to their personal spiritual growth.

Some of these short-term journaling experiences are:

- **Book of the Bible.** The children will concentrate on reading one book of the Bible. Each day they will respond in their journal to what part of that particular book they read. It may be that during the month they'll actually get through the book of the Bible more than once, which will reveal new insights in their second time through. What they write is a response to the love letter God has sent them.
- **God-sightings.** Every day the children will think about how they saw God working in the people or the situations around them. Wow! Wouldn't God love to hear how we see Him in action each day!
- **Prayer.** The kids will actually write—point blank—their prayers and how they see God answering prayer. Encourage them to write to God about their relationship with Him, rather than listing the things they want God to tend to. This is a "Dear God"…journal.
- **I learned today.** This is one of my favorite things to journal. Every day I am aware that God is teaching me something. I'm also learning something new every day. Recognizing that I'm learning about God each day is an exciting thing to write about.
- **Random Scripture.** Take one verse. Read it and respond. Read it again and respond again. These verses don't have to be connected.
- **Spiritual theme.** Show the child how to use the concordance at the back of her Bible. Choose one topic and then read one of the verses listed under that topic each day. Respond to that verse.
- **Prompts.** When you present the child with a blank journal, already have a question written on each page. Make it something fairly general that will allow him to write in a variety of directions.
- **Seasonal.** Journal during the summer, Christmas, or Easter. There are special insights that can come through concentrating on what these special seasons mean in a child's life.
- **Online journaling.** Some sites, like YouVersion, have places on their Bible web sites to keep a personal journal. What a fun way to change things up!
- **Sketch.** Younger children who cannot write fluently may want to sketch their journals. Or, once a week, children can express themselves in their written journal by sketching what they are thinking about.
- **Verbal Journal.** Some children are so uncomfortable with writing that journaling is more of a negative experience than a positive one. There are some options for these kids. Voice-activated journaling is now possible through electronic devices. Using one of these instruments can give a child who struggles with writing the same experience through sharing verbally.
- **Video.** This is a wonderful option for kids who find writing difficult or who are just more verbal. Keeping a video journal can be done in private and has many of the same benefits…if not more. Through video you can also see yourself, your body language, and you can talk faster than you could actually write down the thoughts.

Journaling can be great fun while helping kids grow closer to the Lord. Some kids will latch on to this spiritual discipline with excitement and others will shy away. Your responsibility is to introduce the possibilities and encourage your kids to find ways that help them connect to the One who created them. Journaling is definitely one of those great tools they need to know about!

Prayer Reminders

Objective: To make prayer reminders that help kids develop the habit of praying.

Teachable Moments

Kids need reminders that will encourage them to pray. These reminders are effective tools as little ones develop the holy habit of prayer (or what adults call a spiritual discipline). So, let's look at some little reminders you can use to make prayer a regular part of a child's life.

Before You Begin...

1. **Make a candy countdown rope**. An adult will need to make the tube, but once the tube is made, it can be used multiple times. Armed with a glue gun, you can make one in just a few minutes. And, if you sew, that's probably even better.

   - Cut a 4" wide strip of material.
   - Fold it lengthwise. Hot glue the edges together (or sew).
   - Hot glue one end shut (or sew).
   - If your material ravels easily, turn the tube inside out.
   - Drop a piece of candy into the tube so it goes all the way to the bottom and then twist right above the candy.
   - Tie a piece of ribbon where you have twisted.
   - Drop another piece of candy into the tube and twist. Tie a piece of ribbon.
   - Continue doing this until you have the number you need or you run out of tube.
   - After the tube is made, the kids can actually fill it and will enjoy doing so. Each day, after the child spends time in prayer, she will untie one ribbon and take one piece of candy out. This may sound shallow, but remember we're trying to develop a habit. Once the habit is formed, there's no need for this tube. Hopefully, the child realizes the benefit of prayer without getting a reward. This tube can also be used as a countdown to a holiday/birthday, a reward for inviting someone to Bible School, or motivation to say a memory verse he is working on. And then, when it's empty, just refill the tube.

2. **A stick of gum**. Most packages of stick gum do not have a paper wrapper around each stick anymore; they come with just the foil wrapping. Cut pieces of paper the size to wrap around a stick of gum. On one side of the paper write a prayer initiator. Some of these could be:

   - Pray that you'll have a good attitude throughout your day.
   - Pray about being honest.
   - Pray for 5 people in your class.
   - Pray for those who don't have clean water.
   - Now, wrap this piece of paper around the piece of gum so the words are on the inside. Use a little piece of tape to hold it in place. Each day the child will unwrap a piece of gum and add this prayer initiating thought to their prayer time. And then, chomp-chomp, they get to enjoy the gum. You could also do this around a package of Smarties or other kinds of candy.

3. **Prayer jars**. Write prayer initiators (like above) on strips of colored paper. Roll them up tightly and put them in a decorated baby food jar. They can be taped to keep a tight roll or you can just let them uncoil a little in the jar. This would be a great instrument for family prayer and the jar could be kept on the dining table. When the family finishes their meal, one person can pull out a slip and the family can pray together about that topic.

God Speaks

Now stand here quietly before the Lord as I remind you of all the great things the Lord has done for you and your ancestors. 1 Samuel 12:7 (NLT)

Praying Scripture

From the desk of:
tina!

We want to teach kids to pray according to God's will and one important way to do that is when we teach them to pray scripture. If their assurance is in the Word of God, then they are praying according to God's will. Scripture is God's presence through the written word… how cool is that!

When you use scripture with prayer, it takes what the child has memorized and gives it credibility. You are helping their spiritual growth in a tremendous way! We teach children that if they have scripture stored through memorization in their minds and hearts, then when circumstances arise, they will have their armor available. But, memorizing scripture also has the benefit of helping us pray, knowing the heart of God. We are agreeing with His Word, which releases His power on our lives.

Praying scripture also helps kids have words when they don't really know what to say in a prayer. They can use God's words.

There are a couple of things that help when praying scripture:

- Substitute with "I," "my," "mine," and "me" whenever possible in the scripture to make it more personal. The children will understand that God's Word is truly written to them personally.
- Throughout the scripture, substitute the person's name who you are praying for. This puts a name and face to what God is saying.
- Address God personally. Instead of saying, "The Lord is my shepherd", say, "You are my shepherd, God."
- Say the scripture out loud. Doing this defines each word, and it doesn't just flit through your brain.

When there is a lack of understanding, pray Proverbs 3:5, *I will pursue your commands, for you expand my understanding.*

When you need help, pray Hebrews 4:16, *Let us come boldly to the throne of our gracious God. There we will receive his mercy, and we will find grace to help us when we need it most.*

When someone has done wrong against you and you're having a difficult time forgiving them, pray Luke 6:37, *Do not judge others, and you will not be judged. Do not condemn others, or it will all come back against you. Forgive others, and you will be forgiven.*

When you don't even have words to describe how you're feeling, pray Romans 8:26, *And the Holy Spirit helps us in our weakness. For example, we don't know what God wants us to pray for. But the Holy Spirit prays for us with groanings that cannot be expressed in words.*

Pure Heart Prayer

Objective: To learn how to keep a pure heart by obeying God's Word.

Materials
- Red construction paper
- Black markers
- Scissors

Before You Begin...
1. Show the kids how to fold a piece of red paper in half to make a heart.
2. Once each student has their own red heart, they will write one thing on the heart that they can do this week that will help them keep their heart pure.

Teachable Moments
Do you stay mad at people for a long time and for no good reason? Do you think mean things about certain people? Do you do certain things so that others will notice you and like you? Do you always consider yourself better than other people?

Prayer Time
- Use this sentence to help the children pray for a pure heart.
- Lord, when I (fill in what you have written on your heart), help me remember that You want me to keep my heart pure.

God Speaks
How can a young person stay pure?
By obeying your word and following its rules.
Psalm 119:9 (NLT)

Red Cord Prayer

Objective: To learn that courage is available to us when we pray and ask God for it.

Materials
- Thick red cord
- Red yarn

Before You Begin...
You will need three pieces of heavy red cord cut to 18" each. Hold the ends together and tie a piece of red yarn around the three cords to hold them together.

Teachable Moments
When Rahab hid the spies in the flax on her roof, she showed great courage. Even though she was not an Israelite, she recognized God's power in their midst and believed the God of the Israelites was the One True God. She took a huge chance of being punished severely when she defended the spies instead of turning them in.

As a reward for her courage, she was instructed to let a red rope down the wall from her window, and her household would be protected when the city was attacked.

Courage is what you need when you're going into unfamiliar territory, when you're trying something completely new. It's what you call on when you are different from the people and events around.

Tell about a time when you needed courage. Tell about a time when you didn't have the courage to do something you wanted to do or something you thought you should do.

Prayer Time
- Each time a child shares a reason they need courage, take one of the cords and move it into the braiding position, crossing over another cord. As the needs for courage are shared, a red braided cord will emerge.
- We can help one another have courage and be part of the braid. But, when we bring God into our situation and ask Him for courage, then our braid is "not easily broken" and our fear is not so great.
- Encourage each child to pray a simple prayer about his or her specific need to have courage as you pass around the red braided cord you now have.
- Tie a piece of red yarn around the finger of each child to be a reminder that God will give them courage, just like Rahab received courage because she believed in God's power.

God Speaks
A person standing alone can be attacked and defeated, but two can stand back-to-back and conquer. Three are even better, for a triple-braided cord is not easily broken. Ecclesiastes 4:12 (NLT)

Sandy Prayers

Objective: To discover all the ways and places God is at work in our lives and families—He is enough!

Materials

- Baby food jars
- Colored sand
- Plastic spoons

Before You Begin...

1. Group kids at tables or in circles on the floor. Each group will have a supply of colored sands, and each kid will be given an empty baby food jar.
2. Place a plastic spoon in each color of sand. (It also might be wise to cover the table or floor with a plastic tablecloth, in case sand misses the jars.)
3. If you'd rather not purchase colored sands, you can make colored salt by adding some food coloring to a bowl of salt. Mix it around thoroughly and then lay it out on a cookie sheet to dry completely.

Prayer Time

- We have evidence of God's power around us each and every day. Let's thank God for evidence that He is in charge and at work in our world.
- In each group, the kids will share by saying, "God, I see You real in _____." They can fill in the blank with ways they sense God's presence and see evidence of Him working. Examples: in the way my parents rely on You, in the way You helped my grandma through her cancer, in the change I see in Chris since he gave his life to You, in the way You helped Mr. Helmann when his wife was killed in the awful accident, in the beautiful snow and icicles, in the way You helped my brother get away from drugs.
- Let the kids share how God confirms He is who He says He is and that He is enough.
- Each time someone in the group shares, the kids in that group will all say, "God is enough," and then add one spoonful of colored sand to their baby food jar. Once everyone has a spoonful of sand in the jar, the next person will share. Continue doing this until everyone has a full jar of sand. When we think about all the places where God is at work, it's easy to believe that He is enough for us. He fills us in a beautiful way, just like the sand filled this jar.
- You can use this prayer when you teach the children about John the Baptist in prison. John sent some friends to Jesus; when they returned, they reported what they saw Jesus doing. That was enough for John! That was the assurance he needed to know that Jesus was really who He said He was!

God Speaks

And He has said to me, "My grace is sufficient for you, for power is perfected in weakness."'
2 Corinthians 12:9

Servant Prayer

Objective: To help kids understand that by serving—handing over the treat, praying thanksgiving over the friend, and acknowledging a wonderful trait God put in the classmate—they have exercised their servant muscles.

Materials
- Cupcakes
- Empty chip can
- Napkins
- Pencils
- Strips of paper

Teachable Moments

Place napkins and cupcakes (or another snack) on a table away from the kids. Each child will write his/her name on slip of paper, roll it up, and put it in the chip can.

One at a time, the children will draw a piece of paper from the can and unroll it to see what name is on it. They will go to the cupcake table and pick up one cupcake and a napkin to deliver to the person who is on their slip of paper. As they set the snack down in front of the child, they will say, "Thank you, God, for _____ (child's name). He is _____." Fill in the blank with something positive about the person being served. This isn't easy, because what they really want to do is take the cupcake and run to a corner where they can devour it themselves. They're thinking, "What if all the cupcakes are gone by the time my name is drawn?" By handing over the treat, by praying thanksgiving over the friend, and by acknowledging a wonderful trait God put in the classmate, the serving child has exercised his or her servant muscle. Once everyone is served, they can begin eating.

Prayer Time
- I know you didn't pray for the snack itself! With children (and adults if they'll admit it), it's difficult to make prayer meaningful if they have something tasty sitting in front of them.
- After the cupcakes have disappeared and only the papers are left, thank God for the yummy treat and for the friends who are gathered around the table.

God Speaks

For even the Son of Man came not to be served but to serve others and to give his life as a ransom for many. Matthew 20:28 (NLT)

Sidewalk Chalk Prayer

Objective: To help kids remember the Lord's Prayer by creating murals.

Materials
- Duct tape
- Paint stir sticks
- Poster board
- Sidewalk chalk

Teachable Moments

One of the huge benefits of sidewalks is that they already have areas marked off. And that makes it great for creating murals or separate working areas! When studying the Lord's Prayer, direct the kids to depict different parts of the prayer in sidewalk chalk.

Divide the prayer into the following segments and write them on a piece of poster board. Then, use duct tape to adhere each piece of poster board to a paint stir stick. Place one sign in front of each sidewalk square to indicate what that square will be about.

- Our Father in heaven, may your name be kept holy.
- May your Kingdom come soon.
- May your will be done on earth, as it is in heaven.
- Give us today the food we need,
- And forgive us our sins, as we have forgiven those who sin against us.
- And don't let us yield to temptation, but rescue us from the evil one.

The kids will draw what they think of in each instance. They could also create a rebus to depict the words.

Prayer Time
- When the pictures are complete, ask the artists to be tour guides as they point out what they have drawn and why.
- Pause at each sidewalk square and pray further about each part of the Lord's Prayer.

God Speaks

Our Father in heaven, hallowed be your name, your kingdom come, your will be done on earth as it is in heaven. Give us today our daily bread. Forgive us our debts, as we also have forgiven our debtors. And lead us not into temptation, but deliver us from the evil one. Matthew 6:9-13 (NIV)

Sign-Language Prayer

Objective: To learn to thank and praise God for our strengths and weaknesses.

Teachable Moments

The kids will share some of the weaknesses they have. When do you feel like you just can't do something? Have you ever felt like your teacher or coach picked the wrong person when he or she chose you? We all feel weak when we don't live up to what we think others expect of us or what we expect of ourselves. We also feel weak when there's something in our lives we just can't seem to get past.

Paul felt like that. Apparently, there was some kind of nagging illness that constantly bothered Paul. It made him feel weak. But 2 Corinthians 12:9-10 (NLT) tells us that Paul gained strength when he realized God's response to his weakness was, "My grace is all you need. My power works best in weakness." Paul goes on to say, "So now I am glad to boast about my weaknesses, so that the power of Christ can work through me."

We all need to pray about our weaknesses. We need to hand them over to God and claim His grace and power. When you attack your weakness with prayer, the power of Christ can work through you, just like it did with Paul.

Teach the kids the ASL signs for "weakness" and "strength."

Weak: The fingertips of one hand sit on the palm of the opposite hand, slightly bent. Then, wiggle the fingers back and forth.

Strong: Bend your elbows and pull your fists up to your chest. Your knuckles should be facing out. Then roll both fists forward toward your chest and then outward in a forceful manner.

Prayer Time

- Each time you pray about an individual weakness the kids shared earlier, have everyone make the ASL sign for weak. But, after praying for each weakness, praise God for giving you the strength to go through the situation.
- Now, make the ASL sign for strength. Go back and forth, admitting weakness, then giving God praise for His strength that gets us past our weakness and brings Him glory.

God Speaks

And the Holy Spirit helps us in our weakness. For example, we don't know what God wants us to pray for. But the Holy Spirit prays for us with groanings that cannot be expressed in words.
Romans 8:26 (NLT)

Strength to Accept the Answer

From the desk of: **tina!**

I had been struggling with crippling rheumatoid arthritis since my 18th birthday. Many of my dear Christian friends believed I would be healed and prayed passionately for me. Ray and I constantly prayed that I would be healed. Ministers who had the gift of healing anointed and prayed over me. Nothing. So many spiritual questions to wrestle with.

I grew up hearing the Word of God and being taught that God answers our prayers "yes," "no," and "wait." The reality, though, was that I believed God answers prayer "yes" and "wait." Instead of accepting the "no," I was only willing to admit "wait" for the "yes." Over the years, I've come to realize that's the way most Christians view answers to prayer. When you hear, "God answered prayer," it really means God answered prayer the way someone hoped and wanted. You never hear someone say, "Praise the Lord. God said no!"

Consequently, I lived in "wait" mode for years. Waiting for the day I would play the piano in church again. Waiting for the day I would be whole again and be able to roll on the ground with my toddler son. Waiting for the day the nightmare would be over and I could serve my Lord again. It was physically, emotionally, and spiritually exhausting living in "wait."

One exceptionally pain-filled night, I left our bed to sit out in the living room in our big overstuffed rocker. In the darkness I began talking with the Lord. I cried out for an answer without stipulating the solution I had in mind. I remember saying through tears, "Lord, I don't think I can live in 'wait' any longer. I feel like I'm hanging in space with nothing to grab onto. I need to know 'yes' or 'no.' Am I going to be healed or not? And, Lord, please make me strong enough to handle whatever the answer is."

It was in those moments that I felt God's presence telling me I was not going to be healed. Yeah, God said "no." He assured me He would be right there through everything the future held. There was more, though. He had new plans—His plans—to bring Him glory. Although something seemed to have been taken away, what God put in its place was so much better and made it all more bearable— His joy! Wow! What a gift! MY plans were to be the church pianist/organist and serve as a pastor's wife. GOD'S plans led me into children's ministry. God had much better plans. Nothing against church pianists, but children's ministry rocks!

My "no" answer was just what I needed. I can honestly say that I'm now thankful for my RA. I still hate all the pain and inconveniences that go along with it, but I love what God has taught me on this journey and the new creation He made once I accepted His answer.

My challenge to you is to admit that sometimes God answers "no." Recognize it, teach it to your children, and celebrate that God has given an answer—His answer—even if it wasn't what you had in mind. He knows what He's doing!

Strength Training

Objective: To develop the habit of praying—much like developing strong muscles.

Materials

- Construction paper
- Markers
- Picture of a bodybuilder
- Scissors
- Tape
- Vegetable cans

Teachable Moments

Have you ever seen someone work out with weights? (Show the picture of the bodybuilder.) How do you get muscles like these? You lift a lot of weights… heavy weights…over and over and over again…every day. Little by little, each day the bodybuilder's muscles get stronger. We can strengthen our prayer muscles also—the same way the bodybuilder strengthens his physical muscles—by praying continually, every day, over and over and over again.

Praying continually helps us develop a strong faith. That means you're going to pray at times other than right before you go to bed or before you start eating. Name some other times when you have prayed. When you continually pray, it strengthens your relationship with God, and that strengthens your faith and commitment to Him.

Give the kids a can of vegetables or soup. They will remove the product label, trying to keep it intact. Then, using a permanent marker, they will write on the bottom of the can what is actually inside. Each child will use the label they removed as a pattern to make a similar construction paper label. On this new label kids will write some things they are going to pray about continually. They're going to get lots of prayer exercise because they are going to focus on praying about these situations, such as: a better attitude toward my teacher, showing my brother that I love him, my friend's family because the parents have split, a way for me to help the disaster victims. Now, have them tape the labels onto their cans.

Lead the kids in some calisthenics using their vegetable can before praying. Rather than describing the exercise, instruct the kids to mirror whatever you do with your can. **ASK:** How does your arm feel? Is it a little tingly? Tired? When you first start exercising, your muscles aren't used to all that action. But, each day they will get stronger and you won't get so sore or tired. Prayer is kind of like that too. When you make praying a holy habit, you don't even notice that you're praying about everything that happens in your life. It's just the natural thing to do because you've strengthened your prayer muscles.

Prayer Time

- Ask several kids to pray out loud for one thing they wrote on their can. When they pray, they will lift their can high in the air. If others have something similar they are going to pray about they will also lift their can in the air. As each child prays, continue to hold the cans in the air and add others as they agree with the prayer being led. Send the cans home with the kids for more physical training as they also do prayer training!

God Speaks

Pray continually; give thanks in all circumstances, for this is God's will for you in Christ Jesus. 1 Thessalonians 5:17-18 (NIV)

Take a Hike Prayer

Objective: To learn about directed prayer.

Before You Begin...

1. Prepare some posters with prayer directives on them (like the ones below) that will be posted along the path that you plan to walk.
2. Tack these on trees, steps, railings, or on the sides of buildings.

Prayer Time

For this prayer, you will need to be able to go for a walk. It's best if it's outside, but taking a walk inside the building will also work.

- Pray that God will help you understand His scriptures and that you'll use God's Word as your guide. *Your word is a lamp to my feet and a light for my path. Psalm 119:105 (NIV)*
- Thank God for His beautiful creation that you get to enjoy.
- Tell God how He has made a difference in your life.
- Be still and listen.
- Share with God how you feel when you worship Him.
- Tell God what your favorite song about Him is and why. Go ahead and sing it.

This is a great way to pray at summer camp! The kids can go on their prayer hike individually, following their map, or going by clues you give them to guide them to the next directive. The directives on the signs should encourage the kids simply to talk with God, rather than lay out a "to-do" list of requests they want God to take care of for them.

God Speaks

Your word is a lamp to my feet and a light for my path. Psalm 119:105 (NIV)

Talented Talents Prayer

**Objective: To help kids discover the talents/gifts
God has given them to use for His good.**

Materials

- Biodegradable packing peanuts
- Clear jar with lid
- Play dough
- Water
- Waxed paper

Teachable Moments

Give each child a piece of waxed paper and some play dough. The waxed paper will protect the table surface. What are you good at…really good at? Do you play the guitar well? Are you a whiz at math? Do you know how to take care of plants so they grow healthy and strong? Can you run fast? Are you able to help younger kids understand a difficult subject? Do you recognize when someone needs help, and jump in to help them? Is there something other people often tell you you're good at? Is there something you just really enjoy doing that makes you feel like you did something of worth? Have the kids use their play dough to depict one talent they have.

God gives us special talents so we can use them for His Kingdom. That's the reason God gives us these special gifts! So, look at what you have made from your play dough and think how you could use that talent to bring glory to God. Can you use that talent to help bring people to Jesus?

In Luke 19:11-27, Jesus tells a parable about a ruler who gave three servants some money. Then the ruler went away. Two of the servants used the money they were given to make more. The third servant buried his and didn't use it. When the ruler returned, he was happy with the two servants who had used the money they were given, but he was upset with the man who buried the money he was given. In fact, the ruler was so upset that he took the money away from the third man completely. What do you think that tells us about the talents God gives each of us?

Fill a clear jar halfway with water. Then, put a biodegradable peanut in the water. Tighten the lid and shake the jar. The peanut will disappear. The peanut represents the talent of the third man. When he didn't invest it or try to make more money, the ruler took it away. (An easy place to find biodegradable peanuts is from a Mary Kay distributor.)

Prayer Time

Have the kids cup their hands around what they've made out of play dough as they pray.

My Ruler and my God,

The talent You gave me must be important, because You made it part of who I am. I don't want to be like the servant who buried his money. I want to be like the servants who used what the ruler gave them. Help me to find ways to use the special gift You've given me so that people will get closer to You. Help me get even better at what You've given me as a gift. Thanks for trusting me to use this gift! Amen.

God Speaks

And we pray this in order that you may live a life worthy of the Lord and may please him in every way: bearing fruit in every good work, growing in the knowledge of God… Colossians 1:10 (NIV)

Threshing Floor Prayer

Objective: To find answers from God and confidence from Him when we go to the "threshing floor."

Materials
- Straw or hay
- Tarp

Teachable Moments

In Judges 6, the Bible tells us that the Midianites were terrorizing the Israelites. The Midianites camped where the Israelites could see them, which was very intimidating. Gideon, the prophet of God, went to the threshing floor—a place that was lower than ground level—and hid there. He was threshing wheat when God sent an angel to him. The angel told him to go confront the Midianites, and assured Gideon that God would go with him. But, Gideon had questions for the angel and for God before he had confidence to do what God told him to do.

Before You Begin...

1. Lay a tarp out and spread some straw over the entire covering. This will represent the threshing floor where Gideon was hiding.
2. It was on the threshing floor where Gideon talked with the angel. It was then that Gideon received his orders from God about what he was to do. There on the threshing floor the angel assured Gideon that God would be with him and that gave Gideon new hope for the future of the Israelite people. The threshing floor is where Gideon asked the Lord questions and made his decision of full commitment.

Prayer Time

Bring the kids onto the tarp so they can stand on the threshing floor to pray. Our threshing floor can be a place where we ask the Lord questions; it can be a place of decision if you need to make a commitment. Pose some prayer questions and give the children a few moments to pray about each one.

- Do you wonder why bad things have happened to you or your family? Ask God your questions.
- Do you wonder how God could ever use you? Ask God your questions.
- Do you think of yourself as too weak, too little or too young to do what God asks you to do? Ask God your questions.
- Do you need to make a fresh commitment to worship God sincerely? Make a new commitment to the God who can handle your questions.

God Speaks

I prayed to the Lord, and he answered me. He freed me from all my fears. Psalm 34:4 (NLT)

Time to Listen

Objective: To learn that friendship involves listening as well as talking.

Before You Begin...

Write the following list of questions on a white board:

1. What is your favorite color?
2. What do you like to do after school?
3. What is your favorite place to go?
4. What kind of music do you like to listen to?

Teachable Moments

The children will pair up and ask each other these questions. After a few minutes, discuss how a friendship is formed between two people when you have conversations and find out more about each other. You share information with your friend, and you listen to your friend. It's a two-way street of talking and listening!

Now, call a volunteer to the front of the room. Ask the child the exact same questions that are on the board, but never give the child time to answer. As soon as the child begins to give a reply, rudely interrupt him and tell him your favorite color, what you like to do after school, your favorite place to go, and what kind of music you like to listen to. After interrupting the child during all four questions and only telling your thoughts, tell the child it was nice talking to him and that he is such a good friend.

What was wrong with the way I treated my friend? I did all the talking and no listening. That's the way it is too often when we pray. God calls us friend. He wants to be our friend, meaning He wants to hear from us, BUT He also wants to talk to us! Do you ever sit and listen for God to talk back to you during prayer time? Or, do you do all the talking?

God Speaks

Anyone who is willing to hear should listen and understand! Matthew 13:9 (NLT)

Touch the Globe

Objective: To learn about missionaries all over the world and pray for them.

Materials
- Globe or map

Before You Begin...
- Check out novelty websites like www.orientaltrading.com for different small globe items that can be purchased for the kids as a reminder to pray.

Teachable Moments

Display a large globe or wall map of the world where all the kids can see it and reach it. Identify different countries where your church supports missionaries. When you pray today, the kids can put one hand on a specific country.

Prayer Time
- Encourage them to continue praying for the missionaries in that country this entire week.
- Also, pray that the hearts of the people those missionaries will be talking with will be open to hearing about God's Word.
- Give the children a small globe to take home. When they pray this week, they can hold the globe.

God Speaks

For God so loved the world that he gave his one and only Son, that whoever believes in him shall not perish but have eternal life. John 3:16 (NIV)

Tug-o-War Prayer

Objective: To learn that prayer can help resolve conflicts with others.

Materials
- Large licorice ropes

Teachable Moments

When you are in conflict with someone, you feel like you are being pulled in different directions. The other person doesn't understand why we want what we want. The other person doesn't understand why we have a certain opinion. Or, maybe the other person doesn't understand why we do things the way we do. It doesn't feel good.

When you play tug-o-war, two people or two teams pull in opposite directions. They definitely aren't going the same direction. When we don't get along with someone we love, we feel like we are being pulled apart. Those situations can tear up a relationship.

Think about someone you have conflict with.

Prayer Time
- Divide the students into pairs. Give each pair a licorice rope…the big kind. Each kid will hold onto one end of the licorice rope. When the leader says "go" the pair will gently pull the licorice until it breaks in the middle.
- As you get ready to pray, instruct the children to fill in the blank in the prayer with the name of the person they thought of as they pulled on the licorice.
- Is there someone you're in conflict with right now?
- Pray this sentence prayer out loud and then the kids will repeat it together: *Dear God, help me find ways to get along with (insert name).* All the kids at once will say the name of the person who is on their minds.
- Finish the prayer by praying that each child will figure out how to resolve this or her conflicts.
- Send a piece of licorice home with the kids to remind them of the person or situation they are praying about.

God Speaks

But I tell you: Love your enemies and pray for those who persecute you. Matthew 5:44 (NIV)

Wet Wipe Prayer

Objective: To understand that God is the only one who can clean the messes inside us, and He will.

Materials
- Markers
- Wet wipes™

Teachable Moments

What do you do with a wet wipe? The kids will answer with all the things they can clean with it. It's real good at cleaning up a mess! They're used to clean muddy hands, dirty little baby bottoms, a sticky steering wheel, and the push bar on a grocery cart.

It can clean all kinds of things on the outside, but it can't clean you on the inside. The wet wipe reminds you of all the things that have been dirty but aren't anymore. When you hold a wet wipe, it becomes a symbol for all the dirty things that are now clean.

Prayer Time
- The kids will use a marker to write their prayer on their wet wipe. (A ballpoint pen will not work well.)
- If they have accepted the Lord as their personal Savior, encourage them to write something simple like, "God made me clean."
- If there is a "messy" (stressful) situation in their home or at their school right now, they can write a prayer about that on their wet wipe.
- Or, if God has helped them through a "messy" situation, they can write a prayer of thankfulness on their wet wipe. The kids will hold their wet wipe while they pray.
- End the prayer with, "Thank you God for cleaning us on the inside." Then, rub the wet wipe between your hands (to clean the outside!)

God Speaks

Create in me a clean heart, O God; and renew a right spirit within me. Psalm 51:10 (NIV)

Window Praying

Objective: To learn to pray as Daniel did, with devotion to God.

Materials
- Window crayons

Before You Begin...
1. If you have windows in your classroom you can do this; otherwise, send a window crayon home with each child.
2. Include a note to parents that describes why the child has the window crayon and what he or she is to do with it.

Teachable Moments
King Nebuchadnezzar made a law stating that for 30 days everyone in his kingdom was allowed to pray only to him. No other prayers, no other gods would be tolerated. If anyone chose to go against this law he would be thrown into the lions' den.

Daniel was a devoted believer in the one true God. When he prayed, Daniel was unashamed. He didn't care what other people thought of him. He only knew that he was devoted to God and he loved God so much. Three times a day, he prayed right by his window where everyone could see, even though it was against the law to do so!

Prayer Time
- Give each child a window crayon and remind him or her to ask his or her parents before doing this at home. After receiving permission from their parents, they can use their crayon to write PRAY on their window at home.
- Every time you see your window, I want you to remember how devoted Daniel was to praying, right by his window, three times a day, and how much he must have loved God. This will be a reminder for you to pray and be devoted to God too. If you want to wash it off, you can wash it off easily and it won't hurt your window at all.
- The children could also write their prayer thoughts or requests on their window.
- When they recognize how God has answered each prayer, they can remove them one at a time.

God Speaks
Now when Daniel learned that the decree had been published, he went home to his upstairs room where the windows opened toward Jerusalem. Three times a day he got down on his knees and prayed, giving thanks to his God, just as he had done before. Daniel 6:10 (NIV)

Wisdom Prayer

Objective: To ask God for wisdom for ourselves and others.

Materials
- Crown

Before You Begin...
1. You can use costume crowns (which are really cool), one of the crowns you use for wise men in your Christmas play, or a cardboard crown that you get from the fast food burger place.
2. Or, use one of those cardboard crowns as a pattern to make ones that don't have the logo on them. Decorate with flat-backed rhinestones or sequins.

Teachable Moments

In 1 Kings 3, the Bible tells us that King Solomon had a dream while he slept. In that dream, God told him that he could name anything, and God would give it to him. Wouldn't that be cool! What would you ask God for if He said you could one thing…anything you wanted? King Solomon's reply was different than what you might expect. His kingdom was great and he loved the people, but he wasn't sure he was wise enough to be a good king. So, King Solomon asked God to make him wise. King Solomon wanted wisdom! Why would wisdom make Solomon a better king?

Prayer Time
- James 1:5 tells us that if we lack wisdom we should ask God for it. And what will God do? He will give it…generously…more and more and more!
- Is there a situation in your life right now where you need more wisdom so you can handle it the way God would want you to handle it?
- You can ask for more wisdom…yes, YOU can, just like King Solomon did!
- Set a crown where the kids can get to it easily. If there are kids who realize right now that they need more wisdom and they want God to help them with their situation, encourage them to come up to the crown and put it on.
- Then, they can simply say, "I need more wisdom to _____."
- As they return the crown and go back to their seat, lead the rest of the kids in a prayer saying, "Please God, give _____ more of Your wisdom" (inserting that particular child's name).

God Speaks

"If any of you lacks wisdom, let him ask of God, who gives to all generously and without reproach, and it will be given to him." James 1:5 (NASB)

Wrapped Up Prayer

Objective: To learn that we all need to be more wrapped up in prayer than we are in other things.

Materials

- Markers
- Post-It™ notes
- Safety pins
- Strips of old sheeting

Before You Begin...

1. What does it mean when we say someone is "really wrapped up in _____?" They get extremely focused on a club, a sport, how they eat, what they wear … and so on.
2. Tear some old sheets into long strips about 5" wide.

Teachable Moments

Create groups of 4-6 kids and give each group enough strips so each child has at least one long strip. Each group will choose one child to get "wrapped up" in the strips. Use the safety pins to connect the ends of strips so the wrapping is continuous. There is no need to go around the head, but do challenge the groups to bind the arms and legs securely.

Once each group has a wrapped person, give the kids this assignment. On the Post-It™ notes, write things that kids get wrapped up in. What are you and the kids you know tempted to get "wrapped up" in?

As the kids come up with examples, they will write them on Post-It™ notes. Then, they will stick that Post-It™ on the person in their group who is wrapped. You now have a living, breathing, physical presence of what it means to be wrapped up in something and to be focused on something other than God's plan.

Don't forget the camera! These photos will be priceless. Post them where the adults can see them and wish they were a kid again.

Pull all the Post-Its off your kids who are wrapped up and keep them. Unwrap all the sheeting strips.

Now, choose some of the Post-Its and ask the kids to tell how God can be included in that activity. If you're wrapped up in baseball and nothing else really matters much, how can you change the focus to include God? How can we change our focus in something we're involved in? Our lives are so busy. Sometimes we get so busy and focused on what we're doing we leave God out of our lives.

Prayer Time

- While still in groups, each child will pray, completing the following sentence with the one thing that seems most difficult to include God in. If a kid does not feel comfortable praying, ask him or her to tap the next person on the arm. Dear God, I want you to be part of my _____.

- Go around the group again and have them complete this prayer sentence about the same thing they get wrapped up in. Help me to remember that you are more important than my _____.

God Speaks

Everything is permissible for me—but not everything is beneficial. Everything is permissible for me—but I will not be mastered by anything. 1 Corinthians 6:12 (NIV)

MORE PRAYER IDEAS

Prayer Idea #1

Materials/Supplies
- Baby food jars
- Colored sand
- Plastic spoons

Before You Begin...

   Group kids at tables or in circles on the floor. Each group will have a supply of colored sands, and each kid will be given an empty baby food jar. Place a plastic spoon in each color of sand. (It also might be wise to cover the table or floor with a plastic tablecloth, in case sand misses the jars.)

Prayer Time
- When the friends went back to John, they reported all the wonderful miracles they had seen and God's power was at work through Jesus. We have evidence of God's power around us each and every day. Let's thank God for evidence that He is in charge and at work in our world.
- In each group, the kids will share by saying, "I see God real in _____." They can fill in the blank with ways they sense God's presence and see evidence of Him working. Examples: in the way my parents rely on You, in the way You helped my grandma through her cancer, in the change I see in Chris since he gave his life to You, in the way You helped Mr. Helmann when his wife was killed in the awful accident, in the beautiful snow and icicles, in the way You helped my brother get away from drugs. Let the kids share how God confirms that He is who He says He is and that He is enough.
- Each time someone in the group shares, the kids in that group will all say, "God is enough" and then add one spoonful of colored sand to their baby food jar. Once everyone has a spoon of sand in the jar, the next person will share. Continue doing this until everyone has a full jar of sand. When we think about all the places where God is at work, it's easy to believe—just like John—that He is enough for us. He fills us in a beautiful way, just like the sand filled this jar.

Prayer Idea #2

Teachable Moments

We all come here today from different circumstances. Some of you are facing challenges in your families. Some of you have had the greatest week of your lives. Some of you are full of love, and some are pretty upset with someone. You all come from different places in your spiritual walk: some of you are growing in a close relationship with God, and some of you are trying to figure out how God fits into your lives. Some of you here today might not even be interested in God.

No matter what the differences are, God's grace and love are enough for all of us. (Point to different kids as you say this.) It is enough for you. And, it's enough for you. And, it's enough for you. God wants to fill every single heart with His love, His grace, and His freedom.

Prayer Time

- Have the kids stand in one big circle. A circle shows how we are connected to one another. Each time other persons believe in Jesus as their Savior, they join the circle of believers. God will not allow us to say, "We don't want you in the circle." That's what the Jews were saying to Paul. They were saying, "We don't want the Gentiles in the circle." They were wrong! There's always room for another person. It doesn't matter who they are or what they've done, they can join the circle if they accept Jesus as their Savior. We're connected by God's love.

- While you are assembled in the circle, pray together. Ask each child to put a face in her or his mind—a face of someone that he or she may have judged, may have looked down on. As you pray, the kids should keep that person in mind.

- Heavenly Father, thank You for loving me and giving me Your grace and forgiveness. Forgive me if I have judged someone like _____. Help me to remember that You love everyone and that You sent Jesus for every single person. Although we all go through different things and come from different places, please bring us together to be Your believers.

- Make sure you include the opportunity for a child to make his or her own personal decision to confess his or her sins and accept Jesus as his or her own Savior. You can't share something you don't have. You can't share the good news of Jesus unless you have the good news of Jesus in your own life.

Prayer Idea #3

Materials/Supplies

- Basket
- Pencils
- Scrap paper

Teachable Moments

What do you need to be free of? Do you need to ask God to change your life in a drastic way? Do you need to be set free from the sin you've gotten yourself into? Do you need to come back to the God who created you?

Have you let your mouth say things it shouldn't say? Do you need to be set free from a filthy mouth?

Have you been bullying other kids? Do you need to be set free from having to feel like you're big and bad?

Are you too comfortable with telling little lies? Do you need to be set free from lying?

Are you full of anger at your parents? Do you need to be set free from your awful anger?

We can become a prisoner to all kinds of things, but God wants us to be free in Him. We need to be free of the wrong things so people can see Jesus in us. Write on the paper something that grabs hold of your life and keeps you doing what you know displeases God. What is it you have a hard time shaking? No matter what you write on the paper, God has the power to free you from it, if that's what your heart wants.

Prayer Time

- Give the kids the opportunity to pray a silent prayer about what they wrote on their paper.
- Place a basket in the center of the room, and when they have prayed, they can place their piece of paper in the basket. The basket was how Saul got his freedom from the people who were after him, but his real freedom (and ours too) comes from having a relationship with God.
- Close in a group prayer, asking God to free each person from the things that shouldn't be in their lives. Express the desire to live lives that show Jesus to the world. Amen.

Prayer Idea #4

Materials/Supplies
- Clear jar
- Green pieces of paper
- Pens or pencils
- Rocks
- Water

Before You Begin...
- Fill a clear jar with water. Hold it where the kids can see it. Is this jar full? Yes, it's full to the rim with water. I have a container of rocks here that I want to put in the jar. What would happen if I put the rocks in the jar? The water would spill out. (Feel free to actually do this.)

Teachable Moments
Let's say that the jar is you and the water is jealousy. When the jar is full of water that represents you being full of jealousy. Let's say the rocks are our thoughts and attitudes of gratitude. Each time you add thankfulness to your life, you chase away jealousy. You can't be truly thankful for others and be jealous of them at the same time. It sounds to me like we need to work on being thankful down deep for anyone we're tempted to be jealous of, so those jealous feelings will have to leave.

Give each child a piece of green paper and a pen/pencil. This paper is green, to remind us that even though it's easy to feel jealous, we can GROW in God's grace and have thankful hearts. God wants us to have hearts that are full of thanksgiving, not jealousy. Some of you today are feeling unhappy because you are jealous of someone or something, and you are chasing after the wrong things to make you happy.

Some of you today are always looking for the next thing to make you happy. You might think when you're in preschool, "If only I could go to elementary school, THEN I would be happy. I'm so jealous of all those elementary school students!" Then you might get to elementary school and still be unhappy and think, "If only I could get out of here and go to middle school. THEN I would be really happy! I am so jealous of all those middle school students!" Then you might get to middle school, still be unhappy, and think that high school might make you happy. The cycle could continue on through your whole life. It would be sad if you were never happy because you were always thinking about how happy other people must be and how you wish you could be like them.

Prayer Time
- Today, God can set you free from jealousy. He can change your heart, if you change your focus to Him. Choose to be thankful and grateful.
- We are going to use this green paper to write down all the things we are thankful for. Try to think of as many as you possibly can, and when you can't think of any more, make yourself write down 5 more things. If there is anyone you're jealous of, write down their name and give thanks for them. There's nothing like praising God and praying for people that make us jealous!
- As the kids write and think, pray with them to thank God for all the blessings He's provided. Pray that God will replace jealous hearts with grateful ones.

Prayer Idea #5

Before You Begin...

- Use the flat hands and the fists from Pounding Prayer on page 49 to assist in the prayer time.

Prayer Time

The leader will say a line, and the kids will repeat it, adding their pounding fist or their flat hand to the end of the line. When they pound one fist into their other hand that represents their conflict. When they lay their flat hand in their other hand that represents how God wants them to handle their conflict with His help.

- When I want my way, (pound fist)
- Help me to stop being selfish. (flat hand)
- When I want to come back with a smart remark, (pound fist)
- Help me to keep my mouth shut. (flat hand)
- When I don't consider the feelings of others, (pound fist)
- Help me not to be stubborn. (flat hand)
- When I think I'm better than someone else, (pound fist)
- Help me to remember that we're all the same in Your eyes. (flat hand)
- When someone with the reputation as a troublemaker heads my way, (pound fist)
- Help me to walk away (flat hand).

Amen.

Prayer Idea #6

Materials/Supplies
- Heavy yarn
- Scissors

Before You Begin...
- Beforehand, cut three pieces of thick yarn, each about a foot long. Hold them so the ends are together and then make a knot in the end. This should look like three strands of hair. The kids will make a braid from these three strands before moving into prayer. Each child will also need a pair of scissors.
- When Samson's hair was cut, his strength was gone. When he shared the secret of his strength, he went against his commitment and dedication to the Lord. Each day you have to choose whether you are going to stay strong in your commitment to the Lord or if you are going to fall for Satan's temptations. He knows where your weaknesses are and he will try to wear you down.
- The kids will listen to some of the things that tempt them to turn away from the Lord. If that thing represents something that pulls them away from their commitment to the Lord, then the child should cut off a piece of their yarn braid.
    - o Friends
    - o Habits
    - o Hobbies
    - o School work
    - o Sports
    - o Video games
- When you allow these things to hurt your commitment to the Lord, then you become spiritually weak. God can restore your strength. God can give you new strength when you admit that you've relied on the wrong things for strength. Is your braid chopped up pretty badly? God can give you new strength when you make a new commitment to Him.
- Pray through each one of these areas. The kids may have other areas that cause their commitment to lessen, so include those also.

Even More Prayer Ideas

1. From the News - Find stories in today's newspaper that you can pray about. Then, figure out what you can do to help.
2. Write a letter to God. Then, read it aloud as your prayer.
3. Mad-Sad-Glad (from Generation to Generation by Wayne Rice) Pray for something that you're Mad about, Sad about, and Glad about.
4. Learn four simple motions that go along with a phrase:
   - Life's not (wave hands over one another out from your waist, like the referee signal in football for "no good")
   - about me (thumb pointing at your chest)
   - It's about being Your (point heavenward)
   - servant. (pound fists on top of one another)
   - The kids will repeat these after each prayer statement below that they agree with.

Dear Heavenly Father,
- When I want everyone to look at me, help me remember…(say phrase above with motions)
- When I see someone needing help, let me remember…(say phrase above with motions)
- When I'd like to be honored, let me remember…(say phrase above with motions)
- When I'm upset because I didn't win, let me remember…(say phrase above with motions)
- When helping means doing something that's not fun, let me remember …
  (say phrase above with motions)
- Help me to see that being great in Your eyes means being a servant…
  (say phrase above with motions)
- Amen.

Index

Index of Scriptures

Final Prayer

Please lay your hand on this page.

Dear Father, whose hands are bigger and stronger than any we can imagine, Who reaches where we cannot reach, comforts where we cannot comfort, and hugs when we cannot hug, we are humbled that You love us. As I've put this book together, Lord, I've talked often about the people who would use these pages to bring children into Your presence through prayer. I ask that You fill the hearts of those who desire to place the hand of a child in Your hand and bless them with the satisfaction of knowing they have served You well.

And all the children said…
Amen.

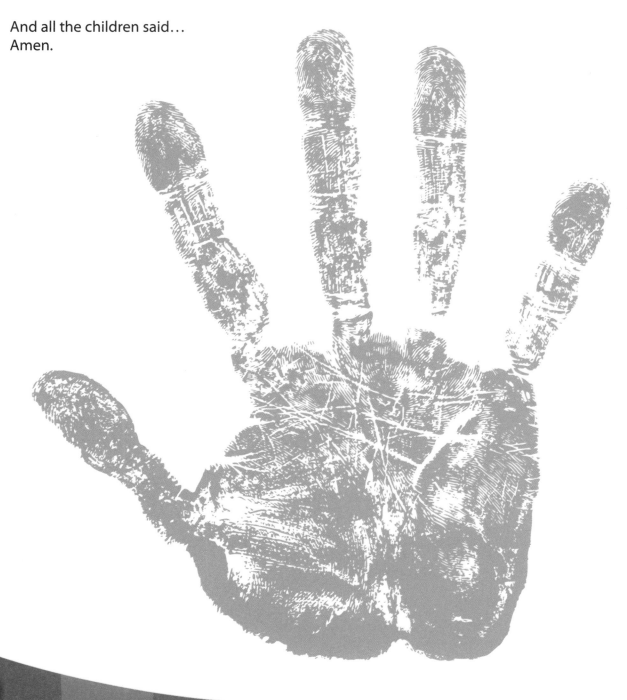